ROM LACK OF ALIGNMENT. LIBERATE FROM "THAT'S HO
YOUR BACK. LIBERATE FROM LEGACY VALUES. LIBERAT
E FROM COMPETITION. LIBERATE FROM FAKE BELIEVE
SS FEARS. LIBERATE FROM CHANGE DRIVING YOU. LIBE
RATE FROM INTERNAL POLITICS. LIBERATE FROM LACK
E IT." LIBERATE FROM WATCH YOUR BA   YOUR
G. LIBERATE FROM CENTRAL N   ERAT
M INACTION & PARALYSIS. LIBE   BU
CONVENTIONAL THINKING. LIB   LEVAN
ALIGNMENT. LIBERATE FROM "THAT'S HOW WE'VE ALWA
TE FROM LEGACY VALUES. LIBERATE FROM CYA THINKI
OMPETITION. LIBERATE FROM FAKE BELIEVERS. LIBERAT
ARS. LIBERATE FROM CHANGE DRIVING YOU. LIBERATE F
RATE FROM INTERNAL POLITICS. LIBERATE FROM LACK
E IT." LIBERATE FROM WATCH YOUR BACK VS GOT YOUR
G. LIBERATE FROM CENTRAL NERVOUS SYSTEM. LIBERAT
M INACTION & PARALYSIS. LIBERATE FROM LURKING BU
CONVENTIONAL THINKING. LIBERATE FROM IRRELEVAN
ALIGNMENT. LIBERATE FROM "THAT'S HOW WE'VE ALWA
TE FROM LEGACY VALUES. LIBERATE FROM CYA THINKI
OMPETITION. LIBERATE FROM FAKE BELIEVERS. LIBERAT
ARS. LIBERATE FROM CHANGE DRIVING YOU. LIBERATE F
RATE FROM INTERNAL POLITICS. LIBERATE FROM LACK
E IT." LIBERATE FROM WATCH YOUR BACK VS GOT YOUR
G. LIBERATE FROM CENTRAL NERVOUS SYSTEM. LIBERAT
M INACTION & PARALYSIS. LIBERATE FROM LURKING BU
CONVENTIONAL THINKING. LIBERATE FROM IRRELEVAN
ALIGNMENT. LIBERATE FROM "THAT'S HOW WE'VE ALWA
TE FROM LEGACY VALUES. LIBERATE FROM CYA THINKI
OMPETITION. LIBERATE FROM FAKE BELIEVERS. LIBERAT
ARS. LIBERATE FROM CHANGE DRIVING YOU. LIBERATE F
RATE FROM INTERNAL POLITICS. LIBERATE FROM LACK
E IT." LIBERATE FROM WATCH YOUR BACK VS GOT YOUR
G. LIBERATE FROM CENTRAL NERVOUS SYSTEM. LIBERAT

PRAISE FOR *RETURN ON COURAGE*

"The difference between mediocrity and greatness or failure and success is one simple ingredient: *courage*. Finding the courage to be different, taking risks, or challenging the status quo are typically our biggest obstacles at work and in life. Thankfully, Ryan provides a playbook to find our inner courage and realize our true potential."

—ERIC RYAN, cofounder, method

"*Return on Courage* is a timely, relevant book that provides the instruction manual for business survival in these turbulent, courage-deficient times."

—JAY BAER, *New York Times* best-selling author, *Hug Your Haters* and *Youtility*

"*Return on Courage* is not only the rally cry that businesses need to stay relevant in today's rapidly changing environment, but it also provides a road map that leads to action."

—NICOLE AYERS, head of innovation team, Nestlé and General Mills, cereal

"Companies are often so busy protecting what they believe they 'own' that they fail to adapt to changing consumers. *Return On Courage* is the playbook to help brands pivot and stay relevant."

—DUSTIN BOMAR, Google, Head of Industry, Travel

RETURN ON
COURAGE

RETURN ON
COURAGE

A BUSINESS PLAYBOOK FOR

COURAGEOUS CHANGE

RYAN BERMAN

GREENLEAF
BOOK GROUP PRESS

Published by Greenleaf Book Group Press
Austin, Texas
www.gbgpress.com

Distributed by Greenleaf Book Group

For ordering information or special discounts for bulk purchases, please contact Greenleaf Book Group at PO Box 91869, Austin, TX 78709, 512.891.6100.

Design and composition by Greenleaf Book Group and Kim Lance
Cover design by Greenleaf Book Group and Kim Lance
Cover image: Lion: Thinkstock / iStock Collection / AOosthuizen

Publisher's Cataloging-in-Publication data is available.

Print ISBN: 978-1-62634-615-4

eBook ISBN: 978-1-62634-616-1

Part of the Tree Neutral® program, which offsets the number of trees consumed in the production and printing of this book by taking proactive steps, such as planting trees in direct proportion to the number of trees used: www.treeneutral.com

Printed in the United States of America on acid-free paper

19 20 21 22 23 24   11 10 9 8 7 6 5 4 3 2

First Edition

To my wife who sits at the center of my Central Courage System®.
To my kids: May you always live courageously.

CONTENTS

THE COURAGE CREDO xiii

Introduction 1

PART 1: A TASTE OF COURAGE 9

    1: The Business Apocalypse 17

    2: The Six Courage Myths 37

    3: Courageously Redefining Courage 51

    4: The Four Principles of Courage 67

PART 2: THE CENTRAL COURAGE SYSTEM 85

    5: Prioritize through Values 89

    6: Rally Believers 111

    7: Identify Fears 129

    8: Commit to a Purpose 151

    9: Execute Your Action 165

    10: Putting It All Together 189

Conclusion: Your Ultimate Return on Courage 193

Epilogue 201

APPENDIX A:
Seven Unwavering Traits of Courage Brands 205

APPENDIX B:
Your Central Courage System Comes with a P.R.I.C.E. 207

APPENDIX C:
Core Values Assessment 211

Acknowledgements 215

Notes 219

Glossary of Terms 229

Index 231

About the Author 241

Inside you breathes an ambitious, inquisitive being yearning to push yourself, your work and your business ahead. You're committed with conviction on elevating your professional trajectory onward, forward, and upward. You're intrigued by the idea of inspiring employees or coworkers to be daring and to think bigger. One thing you know for certain is that the company you work for or your personal brand could benefit from an injection of courage. *That is why this book chose you as much as you decided on it. Let's begin.*

No matter what you are afraid of . . .

THE COURAGE CREDO

COURAGE SETS YOU FREE.

Courage unshackles you from the pack;

it separates you from stuck, risk-averse companies.

Courage is never prejudiced;

It's willingly open for any opportunistic

gender, race, or ethnicity.

Courage *is* a team sport.

There's an *our* in courage for a reason.

Courage can be learned.

So long as you are open to the training.

Courage has a role in your daily life.

It is for **you** and can be your ultimate X-factor.

Above all, courage gets it done.

It stretches budgets further.

And propels you forward, faster.

INTRODUCTION

WHAT MAKES ME qualified to craft a book about courage?

That's a fair question. It's not like I have a lick of military experience. I've never been to Mars or saved someone's life from a burning building. I don't have a PhD, an MBA, or an Ivy League education. Instead, I've been behind the scenes in the field of marketing and messaging for the duration of my career. As a professional story maker, I do know that it takes a bit of bravery to step into the unknown, and when I began this journey, I was delving into unfamiliar territory.

And why would I give up three years of my life to rigorously study courage, or the lack of it, in the business world? Coming out the other side, after conducting a gauntlet of invigorating interviews and digesting vast amounts of research, I now have my answer: This is a story that needs to be told *now*.

There's a noticeable deficiency of courage in the business world. It is absent from business models, boardrooms, company cultures, and mission statements. Courage has, in fact, gone out of style and out of practice—and many businesses are far worse for it.

When I began this 1,000-day deep dive into the subject, I had many questions and a few hunches about the word *courage*. When you start looking under rocks, you're often afraid of what truths you may find.

The good news was that, like most courageous endeavors, I was not alone on this book-writing expedition. When I didn't know something, I went in search of people who did.

I interviewed many bold business leaders for this book, and when approached about the subject of courage, they generously responded, providing me with access to their company's inner workings. From there, I scoured dozens of relevant books, conducted hours of interviews with some of the bravest people on earth, and pledged to learn as much as I could from the resources available to me.

This journey led me to an astronaut; a Navy SEAL; a Cambridge University PhD; a handful of CEOs, company presidents, vice presidents, and chief marketing officers; a *MasterChef* winner; a CNN anchor; an ER doctor; a controversial flight attendant; a few clinical psychologists; a bank teller robbed at gunpoint; and a professional tornado chaser.

What did I learn? You don't have to be an astronaut, a CEO, or a Navy SEAL to have, harbor, or trigger courage.

If you've picked up this book, you've opted in to a community of aspirational, courageous mavericks interested in helping companies survive a tumultuous business landscape. You probably scoff at the idea that anything close to the status quo is satisfactory on your watch. You may have a strong desire to explore the business path less traveled and evolve your company, no matter its size, into perpetual relevancy. Most of all, you understand that companies so focused on being risk-averse are most likely courage-averse.

My hope is that after you finish reading this book you'll come to the conclusion that making courageous business decisions isn't really all that daunting.

We'll demystify the idea of courage prevalent today, redefine the word to those who are willing, and then lead you through a five-step courage instructional manual process I call P.R.I.C.E. **We'll get you properly poised and ready to install courage in your company by first *instilling* courage in your people.** All of this is to help you and your team be better prepared for the realities of an unknown, uncertain tomorrow.

ANGRY. HURT. STUPID.

These were just three of the many colorful adjectives that came to mind when I was let go from a giant New York advertising agency back in 2004.

I was angry because I had given so much of myself to this company over six intensely loyal and devoted years.

I was hurt because I felt that after all this time, they clearly didn't want me, appreciate me, or think I was good enough to be one of them.

And I felt stupid for caring about a place that didn't reciprocate my feelings. They had finally revealed their cards by discarding me into their junk pile.

Looking back, I glowingly ask myself one question about the denouement of my *Mad Men* experience: How is it possible that one of the worst days of my life is now one of the best days of my life?

If it weren't for this agency pink-slipping me, I might still be sitting in that same office strumming up pithy-but-safe 15-second foot fungus animations. If it weren't for getting kicked to their curb, I never would have met my better half, my wife who gave birth to our two beautiful children. I never would have had to cope with real "what am I going to do now" strife, and I know for certain that I would not have had the gall or the courage to become a business owner in this lifetime.

GETTING FIRED WAS MY
NEGATIVE BLESSING

Getting let go from my job, as hard as it was in the moment, made everything else that is meaningful in my life not only possible but also plausible and illuminated.

Just three months later, at 28, I started my first creative agency out of a house with three others. Rather than remaining in the center of the advertising universe on Madison Avenue, we opened our business in San Diego, a place that has long been known for fish tacos, surfing, and sunshine.

We got to work infusing San Diego with a much-needed dose of creativity. And in just five years, we were working with major household brands like PUMA, Bumble Bee Tuna, UNICEF, healthcare giant Aetna, and the Autism Society of America.

You may call it *success;* I call it *getting a return on courage.*

If we could toggle back through a *This Is Your Life* episode of my career, we'd see traces of courage from the get-go, even if I didn't recognize it at play in my younger self.

Back in 1998, as a recent communications graduate, I ambitiously made my way to Manhattan with 22 other hopeful summer interns and arrived at the then 700-person advertising agency Messner Vetere Berger McNamee Schmetterer. The $1.2 billion in billings creative powerhouse, which represented mega companies like Dos Equis, Evian, Intel, Nestlé, and Volvo, was a fierce but thriving learning ground for a kid straight out of college. At the end of the summer, I was fortunate to be the lone intern who landed a job at the agency as an account executive.

I had hoped to enter the creative workforce with pencils sharpened as a copywriter, but instead, I was thrown into an arduous four-year challenge of using the logical and analytical side of my brain rather than my creativity. I assisted business development teams and learned how to steer accounts such as Universal Studios, pharmaceutical giant Schering-Plough, and finally, sandwich king Subway.

With my focus still on fulfilling my goal of becoming a copywriter, I was able to find a handful of mentors at the company, such as James Chung, Eric Bertuccio, and Sam Higgins. They saw that I was passionate about creativity and helped mold me into something better than I ever could have been on my own.

Two years later, with the help of group creative directors Phil Silvestri and Rich Roth, I finally earned my opportunity to use my creativity. You don't find too many account people turning in their window office, button-downs, and khakis for the lowly title of junior copywriter, but that's what I did.

When others doubted my talent, Silvestri and Roth gave me the opportunity to conjure up commercials. Eventually, I delivered. It came in the form of a high-exposure concept—Subway's Jared campaign (before Jared, sadly, became a dirty word). At the time, it was one of the most effective advertising campaigns in quick service restaurant history.

This ad campaign kicked off two high-flying years of traveling to large-scale productions in Toronto, Los Angeles, San Francisco, and Vancouver. I was in constant commercial-making mode, able to shoot with a few high-profile celebrities, like Jaime Pressly and John Madden, while learning and working with some legendary advertising directors, such as Bob Giraldi and Danny Duchovny.

After six years of working at Messner Vetere Berger McNamee Schmetterer, I had achieved what I had set out to accomplish and more. With my goal realized, I vividly remember thinking to myself, *What next?*

Before I could tackle that question for myself, a new executive creative director was hired and answered it for me. My pink slip now in hand, my "what next?" abruptly morphed into a daunting "what now?" Unbeknownst to me at the time, that's when courage truly kicked in.

Seven years of success with my first San Diego start-up, Fishtank, led me to merge that company into my next creative venture: an integrated agency called i.d.e.a. With my two cofounding partners, we solved problems for such companies as Caesars Entertainment, Hostess Brands, Major League Baseball, Qualcomm, St. Regis Hotels, Fender guitars, U.S. Ski & Snowboard Association, and Curio Hotels.

During my time as a business owner, I had the good fortune of selling above-the-noise effective advertising in every corner of the country. My agencies had conjured up stories with David Hasselhoff, William Shatner, pro golfer Rickie Fowler, Segway inventor Dean Kamen, skateboarding star Nyjah Huston, a handful of contortionists making up a Human Motorcycle, a few electrifying elephants, and a Movember hand puppet. It's all part of a normal day in the life of an abnormal occupation.

The charismatic Grant Cardone, author of *The 10X Rule*, said it best, "Nothing happens to you; it happens because of you."[1]

EITHER CHANGE DRIVES YOU OR YOU DRIVE CHANGE

Change drove me out of a fast-paced New York work life and my comfort zone into the world of entrepreneurship. Besides thinking about my friends or the Chinese food, I've never looked back—with the exception of reminiscing about the little gift I've coined as my negative blessing, getting fired.

Perhaps your negative blessing is lurking right around the corner—an acquisition made by your closest competitor or, personally, a promotion that you didn't get. When you are faced with change, do you step up and accept the circumstance or do you allow yourself to be a victim of this newfound reality?

Whether you're a CEO, a vessel for change, or just entering the workforce, I wholeheartedly believe consciously choosing courage works wonders for any willing soul. Unlocking courage, when truly embraced and understood, can be your competitive advantage and ultimate X factor—not just at your current job but also throughout your career.

Let me show you how.

A Taste of Courage

YOU DON'T NEED much courage to earn a pay raise or climb the corporate ladder. Rather, the opposite is usually true; it's better to play it safe. Why stick your neck out if there's a chance you could get yourself fired? Why put your reputation on the line when you can be penalized, if you're not careful, for doing so? This is the reality of many "It's just a job," fear-based business cultures.

In today's workplace, most of us are not compensated for courageous feats. Instead, we are rewarded for staying the course and remaining in the safe zone. Going outside of that is a risk and could uproot your livelihood. And this, most likely, won't affect just you. There are families at stake. The bigger the family the smaller the amount of risk you may be inclined to take in the workplace.

This shows us just how broken our business culture is and how absent courage is from it. We do whatever we can to protect ourselves—at all costs—regardless of what's best for the business. The company is compensating you for great leadership, great thinking, great creativity, great management, and great results . . . and you're only thinking about protecting yourself.

Well, we are human.

But what happens when you decide that the corporate status quo is not enough? What potential could be unlocked if you commit to putting that business before yourself? What could the future of your company look like with a calculated infusion of courage?

Let's take, for instance, a 50-year-old Michigan pizza company that was still using its original recipe and suffering from poor customer satisfaction and debilitating sales. This was the gloomy reality back in 2008 for pizza delivery giant Domino's.

"When I joined Domino's at the end of 2008, we had just come off three consecutive years of negative sales," says Russell Weiner, who served 11 years at Pepsi before coming on board as a first-time chief marketing officer at Domino's. "A decent portion of our franchisees weren't even breaking even, and the stock price was as low as $2.84. It was a mess."[1]

Not only was the stock price a mess, there was reason to fear the product didn't cut the mustard. When your "product fear" revolves around taste, and yours is perceived as subpar in the industry, you have a major problem on your hands that can't simply be solved in 30 minutes or less. A bad-tasting recipe is the nail in the coffin for any restaurant business. It was clear, however, that Domino's not only had product issues but also a perception problem.

"We did not rank high on product scores. But believe it or not, people thought our product tasted better when it was in somebody else's box," Weiner says. "And, vice versa, their products tasted worse when they were in our box."

With that can't-win situation, Domino's was in serious trouble.

As the old marketing adage goes, "Nothing kills a bad product better than good marketing." So Domino's began to put in the legwork to address its product fear head-on. The company secretly conducted two years of product research and in 2010 courageously dropped the five-decades-old recipe to launch a completely overhauled Domino's pizza.

"It's not a slight tweak," the then Domino's USA president J. Patrick Doyle said at the time. "We changed everything on our pizza from the crust up. We changed the crust; we changed the sauce; we changed the cheese."[2]

Weiner remembers: "We blew up the bridge. We had courage obviously to do that, but it also put us in a situation where we had to be all-in. We needed to create five years of sales in one year, which meant we needed an incredibly strong message. If our message was strong though, our product needed to be great."[3]

With the ingredient upgrades, Weiner believed Domino's had upped its taste game. Testing showed that its pizzas tasted significantly better than the competition's.

With the taste problem now a taste advantage, Weiner knew he could be riskier with addressing the perception fear through the company's communication strategy. He took what he learned by listening to employees, customers, and critics and developed a plan to bring the truth to America through commercials. The script was to paint an honest portrayal of how Domino's had heard its critics loud and clear. The company was owning up to its mistakes and responding by transforming just about everything about itself to create a new, better pizza.

What the Domino's marketing team created for the public was one of the most successful campaigns in restaurant history: "Oh Yes We Did."

"I didn't know at the time, but when I went to pitch the idea to our CEO Dave Brandon, he was about to retire," Weiner says. "If you're him, knowing that you're going to leave, you probably say, 'Hey, you know what? Don't do something so risky. Just say, new-and-improved Domino's, and you'll be up 2 percent.' He OK'd this thing. The guy that took his place, Patrick Doyle, who's still our CEO, I put him in the ad. It could have been career enders for everyone."

The night before the campaign broke, Weiner recalls that he wasn't worried about the much-improved taste of his product. He was concerned the world wasn't truly ready for what Domino's was about to say. "I actually got nervous, because I realized I had just lived every marketer's dream. They let me do exactly what the team thought was the right thing to do. It's nobody's fault but ours if this fails."

When the campaign first aired, Weiner instantly received a call from one of his franchisees. "He was like, 'This may be a job for you, but this is my life. You just said our pizza sucked.'"

Can you imagine the horror experienced by many of these franchisees, who were terrified that the results of what Weiner had done might unhinge their jobs and families?

The good news for Weiner was that his return on courage was almost instantaneous. The "Oh Yes We Did" campaign instigated an immediate positive impact on Domino's bottom line.

"Our 24-hour sales were so crazy. After the second week, we were two days from running out of pepperoni. In fact, we were up 9.9 percent for the year, and perhaps if we would have been staffed right to answer the phones, we could've been up another two to four points."

Since the campaign launched in 2010, according to Weiner, Domino's is the fastest-growing major restaurant company. Franchises are making money, as are stockholders. The stock price has come a long way from a paltry $2.84 when Weiner joined the team to sitting now at just over $270 a share. In fact, since the relaunch, Domino's stock has outperformed a handful of giant tech companies, including Apple, Tesla, Netflix, and Google.[4] Not bad for cheese, dough, and sauce!

Weiner still gives most of the credit to Brandon and Doyle and sees them as the real courageous ones in the scenario for believing in Weiner and his team's recommendation.

"As you move up in your career, it's more and more difficult to be courageous, because you're far removed from the actual data," Weiner says. "Here, our president and CEO had trust in the marketing guy and his team who were telling them the data was real. Their response was, 'All right, pull the cord.'"[5]

To be courageous you have to be able to put your trust in others. Courage is a team sport, and no one exemplified this better than the senior team at Domino's.

Weiner confesses: "I think 95 percent of leaders would have thrown me out with what was a huge campaign change for us. I might have thrown myself out, to be honest."

Domino's combated its product fear by upgrading its 50-year-old pizza recipe. Then it used marketing to shrink its perception fear with a virtuous campaign. "Oh Yes We Did" remains a powerful and purposeful guidepost for Domino's today.

Whether you work for an established business with a critical, looming decision to make or a Silicon Valley start-up looking to set up a company the right way, I hope you will use the insights outlined in *Return on Courage* to help you.

1. **Maximize your return on investment.** I asked myself if organizations could proactively prepare themselves to thrive in a business world with an uncertain future. And because of my research on this daring topic, I am convinced the answer is a resounding yes—with courage. When you drive change, when you have the courage to not simply survive but *transform*, I believe there is an immense, amplified return on your efforts. When you set yourself up to make and follow through with calculated, bold choices, like

Domino's did, return on courage (ROC) is the ultimate way to catapult return on investment (ROI). The positive impact these decisions produce reverberates throughout your own organization and the outside world.

2. **Return to relevance on the courage platform.** From time to time, you may hear people throwing around the term *legacy brand* to describe a business that has been around for a long time. Many times, this means it's a dying brand. These brands have often drifted off course and need new life breathed into them. They have to want to be helped, and if they willingly commit, the process put forth in this book can turn their behemoth boat around before it's too late. If you are going to make a comeback, you have to follow through. Domino's proved that no matter what kind of business you're in, how many decades you've been operating, where you are headquartered, or the size of your company, you can return on the courage platform.

Most corporations are focused on mitigating risk. When they do this, perhaps unbeknownst to them, they are also mitigating courage. Those who are risk-averse are inadvertently courage-averse. And for those companies where risk has been readily accepted in business, courage has often been disappointingly rejected. Most businesses have regular meetings in which they talk about risk. Rarely do you see discussions about courage. We need to return the word *courage* back where it belongs—in the business lexicon.

Myron Scholes is a former professor at Stanford, MIT, and the University of Chicago. He's also an expert on risk, having won the Nobel Prize in economic science for his groundbreaking studies on the subject. "We all have a taste for it," he says. "In life, it would be kind of boring if there was no risk. On the other hand, if there's too much risk, too much uncertainty, too much chaos, we can't handle it either.

We simultaneously want order and disorder, simultaneously want risk and quiescence."[6]

It's time to reject the idea that courage has little to no role in the workplace and accept the necessary balancing act between risk and courage.

If courage is the accelerator, then risk is the brake pedal. You need them both to drive a car, but you can't press them at the same time or the car won't work. In the end, hitting the accelerator is what makes the car go. So the question becomes, "How hard should you hit the gas?"

What we're really talking about here is a willingness to change. What if we could instill in you the necessary training to make courageous decisions in your business? What if you were empowered with the tools you needed to be a bold force for positive, evolving change in your workplace?

It's time you unlocked courage within your company, your product, and your marketing. It's critical you do everything in your power to make a relevant return now to the conversation.

Courage is most definitely for *you*. Courage is for your direct manager who may be suffering from symptoms of indecisiveness. Courage is for the CEO who is doing her best to navigate the leadership team, board of directors, or Wall Street.

Courage is not something that should be used only by the most senior people in businesses—it is for your whole team and an essential advantage to be harnessed when taking on tomorrow's tumultuous business landscape. How terrifyingly bad is it out there?

I call it the Business Apocalypse.

THE BUSINESS APOCALYPSE

THE QUARTERLY REPORT unveils your truth. It's out there for the world to see, and it is as disappointing as the current tepid share price. While the stock continues its free fall, layoffs and internal strife are on the rise. Working capital is waning, and the bleak tone on the recent earnings call said it all.

Your company has cancer.

The toxicity is spreading noxiously throughout your organization from one department to the next.

You're probably in shock that something like this could happen to you and your company. And at this point, energy is fleeting. You have a hard time doing or thinking about anything else. You don't know *if* your business will survive, what your company's quality of life will be, or how long it will live—if it lives.

All you know for certain is that what's happening to your business is very real, and you can't run from this gloomy prognosis.

Being aware of this certainty means that you can no longer ignore the warning signs you see happening around you.

That's when it dawns on you: *You have a choice.*

You can build a foundation to help turn your business around. You'll need committed internal support ready to go the distance with you. You can fight this business cancer head-on, but you must be dedicated, willing, and able to combat this horrific reality.

The choice is yours: You either battle this business cancer like mad or simply succumb to its pressure.

Thomas Purcell helps patients combat cancer in real life. Trained at Johns Hopkins, Purcell is the oncology system director at the University of Colorado Hospital. As an oncologist since 2002, he sees patients in the lung and gastrointestinal clinics.

"It can be hell," he says. "I don't think we do enough to assure cancer patients how courageous they are."[1]

Just like in business, cancer fighters are taking on a variety of difficult situations, including the cost, the burden on their support network, and of course, the unknown outcome.

"Most want to fight," Purcell says. "The question is, are they capable of fighting? Or has the cancer made them so weak that they can't mount a charge?"

One thing Purcell makes clear is that for cancer patients to face the battle ahead, they need to commit to making the necessary changes in their life that are under their control.

"You really can't control whether or not the chemo is going to work," he says. "It either is, or it isn't. What you can control is your nutrition, your fitness, and your determination to stay strong, keep your stamina, and maintain your weight. You can control whether you are putting yourself in the best possible position to receive the next treatment."

The same is true in business: You must be prepared. Although you can't control outcomes when change drives you, you certainly can do your part by driving the change.

Purcell says, "A fit patient is going to do better than a person who is not fit. So, if you are motivated and you want to stay strong, you need to put the extra effort into what is under your control—staying fit. This way, you will get better outcomes."

Unhealthy businesses are often hesitant in their decision making because they aren't prepared to make these decisions, and without a plan in place, they don't stand much chance for survival.

By no means are business complications as heart-wrenching as seeing a loved one struggle with cancer. But one thing that is similar about these situations is that many of us believe that these circumstances happen to other people—never to us or someone we know.

In business, it's about being aware that this happens more times than it doesn't. So what will you do to proactively keep your organization fit, your business model healthy, and your brand in shape?

THIS IS THE DAWN OF THE BUSINESS APOCALYPSE

Fifty-two percent of the Fortune 500 companies from the year 2000 are now *extinct*.[2] That's not a typo. In less than two decades, more than half of the brands that were on the Fortune 500 list in 2000 no longer exist.

Fifty years ago, the life expectancy of a Fortune 500 brand was 75 years; now it's less than 15.[3] It has been predicted that an estimated 9,000 companies could find their way on and off the Fortune 500 list over the next six decades.[4]

The Business Apocalypse has caused the demise of many once-thriving corporations. Companies we used to adore like Toys "R" Us, Tower Records, Pets.com, Blockbuster, and Kodak are no more.

So what's causing all this? And how can your company avoid this grave danger? I believe it starts by first accepting the **Four Truths of the Business Apocalypse:**

1. Companies are perishing at an alarming rate.

2. We are afraid of change.

3. What got you here won't keep you here.

4. You need time, but you don't have time.

These truths are daunting, but instead of suppressing them, it's time to acknowledge them and take action. We must work closely with our teams to shift their mentalities from "There's no time like the present" to "There's no time *but* the present." When you do, you can decrease your company's chances of falling to one of these statistics. But you must have the courage to do so.

Let's start by unpacking the first truth.

Truth #1: Companies are perishing at an alarming rate

A recent white paper released by the Boston Consulting Group reported that public companies of all shapes, sizes, and sectors are going out of business at an alarming rate. Assessing 35,000 listed corporations since 1950, the study noted, "Public companies have a shorter life span now than ever."[5] To make matters worse, as quoted in the same study, "Businesses aren't just dying off sooner. They're also more likely to perish at any point in time." This is the dire truth of business today. Big business, small business, brick-and-mortar retail stores, and apparel companies are all vulnerable. No business is safe.

But why is this?

Let's return to the good old days when there were fewer choices. Say you wanted to buy yourself a new jacket. There were only a few companies selling them and just a couple of stores you could walk into to try one on for size. You had to go to the store to get the jacket, and you couldn't just walk in when you wanted to because these stores kept limited hours.

These jacket companies relied on a handful of traditional ways of advertising to make you aware of their offerings. Back then, the benefits of the jacket were nothing more than keeping you warm and matching your style. Things were simpler then.

Today, there are scores of jackets on the market and dozens of ways these companies are making you aware of them. Thanks to the Internet, anyone can effortlessly purchase a jacket online, around the clock; summoning the jacket directly to you.

Thanks to technology, the capability now exists for you to virtually see what you look like in that jacket—all 360 degrees—just by uploading your picture through the corporate website or mobile app.

The jacket, which once just had to keep you cozy, for many, now has to be crafted with a certain type of eco-friendly quality to qualify as cool in the eyes of a cause-centered generation.

More choices. More noise. More access. More qualifiers. More than ever, every moment of every day is an opportunity for a competitor, currently known or unknown, to swoop in and sway your customers away.

Business has changed. The paradigm has shifted; it used to be enough to get customers to just buy the things you were selling. Now, you need customers who *buy in* to your company as a whole. The digital revolution has provided consumers with access to information they once did not have, and businesses must be more transparent today than ever before. Now, values-based, socially responsible, and purpose-driven companies are here to stay. These are the types of companies that are winning today's business game.

Many traditionally run companies remain stuck playing by the old rules of business. They are hesitant to pull the trigger and commit to these newer practices, products, and perceptions, and they are struggling to stay relevant in a rapidly changing, fast-paced world.

No one seems to be feeling this worse than retail. Even malls as a whole are going away. Twenty-five percent of all malls are predicted to disappear, vanished from the earth, in just a half decade. "RetailFail" is here to stay as digitally native brands continue to eat share from the old guard. The mass offline-to-online shopping movement is very real, and there's no surprise that Jeff Bezos is smiling because he has millions of happy, reliable, and consistent repeat customers all over the country. Sadly, Amazon's successes, as we've now learned, breed seismic setbacks for plenty of legacy brands.

It's not just the older companies that are dying, though; new businesses are having their own share of troubles as well—95 percent of all new companies don't survive their first decade,[6] while 80 percent of start-ups are failing within 18 months.[7] Steve McKee, author of *When Growth Stalls,* has research suggesting that "some 90 percent of the thirty thousand brands launched each year fail."[8]

Because of this, people are perhaps more hesitant to start businesses. Though there is some chatter predicting an entrepreneurial bounce back, the Ewing Marion Kauffman Foundation reports that "America has been living in a long-term decline of entrepreneurship." In response to this reality, Kauffman Foundation President and CEO Wendy Guillies said, "This needs to be a national wakeup call. The long-term decline is eating away at America's spirit and competitiveness." She continued, "As a nation, we must re-create the conditions in which optimism can thrive."[9] It takes courage to go out on your own, and people have been doing it less and less over the last half decade.

This grim state of business, across the board, is very real. It is no longer business as usual; it's only business as unusual.

Author and researcher Jim Collins writes near the end of his book *Great by Choice*, "Instability is chronic, uncertainty is permanent, change is accelerating, disruption is common, and we can neither predict nor govern events . . . We believe there will be no 'new normal.' There will only be a continuous series of 'not normal' times."[10]

How abnormal could it get? Former Cisco CEO John Chambers predicted in 2015 that 40 percent of *all* companies could be dead in a decade.[11]

Is the sky really falling? Is the instability of the current business climate why SpaceX CEO Elon Musk is relentlessly pursuing life on Mars?

The reason for this proliferation of business casualties can be broken down into external and internal factors.

External Factors

Companies have more competition, fight more noise, and have less control than in the good old days. Customers have more access to products, but they devote less time and are less swayed by brands and by advertising than ever before.

Today, we have more TV channels to surf, more websites to peruse, more shoe companies to consider, more beers to imbibe, and more food, books, and toys that can be swiftly delivered to our doorsteps (quite often, on the same day we purchase them). We have more access to people's opinions, more ways to quickly see if a restaurant is "Yelp-worthy," and more screens to consume it all on. With more data, more friends—real and social media—we now have more "more" than we know what to do with.

The noise is deafening, as every minute of every day we perform 2.4 million Google search queries, upload 300 hours of YouTube videos, and post more than 31 million Facebook messages around the globe.[12] As a business it has never been harder to be heard.

With so much available information that they now control, consumers are in the driver's seat calling the shots. If business took place on a tennis court, it used to be all serve by the business and no volley by the customer. Now, thanks to social media, you can watch the conversation between businesses and consumers rally back and forth. If a customer hits a scorcher over, a business has the opportunity to zing a return comment. However, if a customer desires, they get to take that last parting shot. And the business may have to live with it—even when the shot lands out of bounds.

Customers have more access to information today than ever before, and with this access, comes speed of information. Where it took 38 years of radio to reach 50 million people, it took less than 38 days for Angry Birds to saturate screens and nab the same number of users. The telephone reached 50 million users over 75 years; Facebook matched that in 3.5 years.[13]

Meanwhile, with all that access to noisy competition, consumers are taking less time to decide what is and isn't right for them. Consumers have around-the-clock options at their fingertips, but the amount of time businesses have to grab their attention continues to dwindle. In the '90s, brands had up to 15 minutes to make their case; now attention spans are as limited as the amount of time it took to read this sentence.[14]

Not only are customers giving you less time, but they're also less swayed by your messages. For one, they don't really want to hear from you—unless you messed up. (And in those cases, they want to hear from you as fast as possible.)

Many younger people are blocking ads altogether. eMarketer reported that 63 percent of Millennial males are using an ad blocker.[15] eMarketer forecasted that ad blockers could be the best friend of nearly 30 percent of *all* Internet users by the end of 2018.[16]

If businesses are blocked, they can't sway potential customers the same way they once did. Case in point: Fifty percent of all television viewers under the age of 32 will not subscribe to a traditional pay TV service by 2025.[17] This would make TV commercials obsolete.

With customers having all this newfound control—including

access to price information and real-time peer commentary—one has to wonder if many of our staunch, dependable customers are becoming less loyal to brands they were loyal to in the past.

We don't have to wonder, it's true. In today's what-have-you-done-for-me-lately society, people are no longer as faithful to certain brands. As much as businesses wish customers acted like dependable owners, more times than not, next generation customers behave like renters—renting a brand before moving on to a better option when they see one.

In some ways, it's easier for start-ups to compete these days. Most of these companies that get to start from scratch are building contemporary businesses that cater to this new kind of consumer from the very beginning. Imagine you are house shopping. If you had to pick between an antiquated fixer-upper built in the 1950s versus a modern home built this year, which would you choose? The competition entering the market has less baggage than traditional business models do.

If there is a silver lining here, it is that a majority of all businesses are dealing with these same external factors, which brings us to the organizational health headaches brought forth from a slew of complicated internal factors.

Internal Factors

Many leadership teams would like nothing more than to shortcut the process professing change to the external world without truly committing to the hard work it takes to internally change an organization. Let's take a moment to remember our case study on Domino's. It took Weiner and team two years of revamping their product before they were able to courageously communicate these modifications to the outside world.

For companies that need to reconsider their business model to stay relevant, often they first need to look within and make changes in their own company. Easier said than done. A lot of friction comes with internal change in organizations, and it can be particularly difficult with employees who are too self-serving, too proud, too skeptical, or in denial.

Simply put, internal change is hard, and it's made even more difficult because of the speed bumps of interoffice politics and mass hierarchy.

An organization is a conglomeration of individuals, and the way those individuals come together and interact is an organization's culture.

There is almost nothing more disruptive than trying to shake up a well-established culture. It's not as if we can just buy a newly aligned culture from Amazon and have it shipped overnight to our businesses' doorstep. Changing a company's culture takes time and effort because there are so many different personalities involved.

Say your CEO still listens to Queen. Senior leadership sings in the car to Prince. Meanwhile, your salespeople's headphones blast Kings of Leon. When there are so many different kinds of people with their own opinions and preferences, there is bound to be a culture clash.

When your culture needs a makeover, you have to confront it, discuss it, and work at it.

Retired IBM CEO Louis Gerstner wrote in his book *Who Says Elephants Can't Dance?*, "I suspect that many successful companies that have fallen on hard times in the past—including IBM, Sears, General Motors, Kodak, Xerox, and many others—saw perhaps quite clearly the changes in their environment. What I think hurt the most was their inability to change highly structured, sophisticated cultures that had been born in a different world."[18]

Internal change is risky, and many variables must be considered. When a company does decide on internal change, a strategy is usually developed that can be implemented gradually. Many people adhere to the philosophy that it's slow and steady that wins the race. Deviating from that strategy, even when you don't agree with it, can be perceived as catastrophic.

Personal risk makes it hard for us to speak our minds. It's especially difficult to put your reputation on the line once you've received approval from superiors on a proposed change. What we need to remember is that, like the stock market, life fluctuates. What was the right decision for your business a month ago may not be the right one today. There is always new information to consider or even how the business landscape is evolving in real time.

This doesn't mean we should be altering our strategy every time the wind blows. It means we should be open to those truths by looking for the changes around us and granting our people leeway to alert us of those changing truths as well. Honest, agile communication is the key. Even if you reached consensus just weeks earlier, if you believe changing your game plan is the right thing to do, then you should bring it to your team's attention. This, of course, can be embarrassing or painful to fulfill when you do have an ego and you don't have trust.

When you do have that trust, you can take more risks in implementing and instigating radical corporate internal change. Without putting an emphasis on change, without evolving your business, you are nothing more than an idle company at risk. To stay the course for the sake of staying the course is not a reason to avoid hard internal conversations.

Manny Rodriguez, chief marketing and experience officer at University of Colorado Hospital, agrees. "Just because something worked yesterday doesn't mean we're going to do it the exact same way tomorrow," he says. "There's a lot of *well, we've always done that.* I literally had an argument with a physicians group because they're like, 'Well, our competitors do it.' I replied, 'Just because they're stupid, doesn't mean we need to be stupid.'"[19]

Today's best practices are tomorrow's problematic, outdated processes.

Changing is hard, and changing quickly is harder. Zappos CEO Tony Hsieh knows the businesses that are too slow to change are quite often the first ones to put themselves in the line of fire. Hsieh builds off the ever-so-famous Darwin thought when he shares, "A well-known tenet related to biological evolution is that it is not the strongest, or fastest, or most intelligent of species that survives . . . It is the one that is most adaptable to change. I believe the same is true for companies."[20]

Injecting a sense of urgency into a sensible plan is the potential path to resolving the problem of internal paralysis. Much easier said than done. Even when a company commits to making change, few corporate initiatives are ever successfully implemented.

The management consulting company Accenture came to a similar conclusion in its 2015 US Innovation study. American executives and managers were asked about their companies' attitudes toward innovation. Sixty percent agreed or strongly agreed that their organization struggled to learn from past mistakes. More than 70 percent agreed or strongly agreed that opportunities to harness underdeveloped areas died because companies couldn't find an internal home to nurture them.[21]

Then there's the internal killer of employees being too self-serving.

Brian Enge is the CEO of Robin Hood Brands, which is a new company that sells factory-to-consumer brands primarily on Amazon. Previously, Enge spent three and a half years as president of Southern California performance athletic training company SKLZ. When Enge thinks of workers as a whole, he believes, "We're in this real funk right now and have been for the last decade," he says. "Too many people are in the business of job preservation."[22]

Enge believes we should be in an era of personal responsibility, but behavior proves otherwise: "I have friends running companies of all shapes and sizes. This wasn't merely a SKLZ problem. It's an every company problem. Many want to blame someone else and deflect personal responsibility. Ultimately, you have to be responsible for the things you do."

Some people are in the business of getting ahead while many are, sadly, in the business of preserving their status quo.

Which brings us to those employees who are simply too proud. In this rapidly changing business climate, it's important to be able to admit when you don't know something and ask for help.

Jason Spero is a vice president of performance media at Google. He's focused on the developing changes taking place in the ad tech, mobility, and media worlds.

With roughly three million marketers as clients, Google and Spero have observed a wide range of partners, spanning from the largest Fortune 50 all the way down to small businesses like flower shops and hair salons.

"I would say that anybody who's got a website is finding it challenging," Spero says. "The vast majority of the chief marketing officers who I deal with are feeling unsettled about how ready they are for the current wave of consumer behavior, and they need a lot of help."[23]

Spero suggests that while many of his larger clients ask questions when they don't know something, a handful of his other clients are often afraid to vocalize that they simply don't know.

"If we're just talking about the top 2,500 clients, I would say most of them are pretty good at asking for help," he says. "That doesn't mean that they admit weakness or that they overcome some of their organizational biases and inertia. The ones that are proud probably don't ask for the help, and they're both scratching and clawing to try to keep up with the pace of change."

Our pride makes it difficult for us to pull the trigger on decisions because it could hurt our reputation or personal ego.

Pride can sometimes get the best of even the most successful entrepreneurial super humans. Jay Coen Gilbert, who cofounded and sold shoe giant AND 1 for more than $250 million, dealt himself a harsh critique. "I didn't have the courage to not be CEO when I should have realized that I was not the best person to run the company," he says. "I didn't have the courage to tell my ego to go take a seat."[24]

The sum of these internal factors (employees being too resistant to change, too self-serving, too proud, or too much in denial) and external factors (fighting off more competition, more noise, and more access to real-time information thanks to mobile phones) is the leading contributor to this corporate casualties epidemic.

Truth #2: We are afraid of change

Nicholas Alp is an interventional academic cardiologist who earned a PhD in immunology at Cambridge University. Alp has two decades of clinical research experience under his belt and has been published in more than 60 peer-reviewed periodicals and books.

"If we think about the fundamentals of staying alive on this planet, and the evolutionary pressures that helped to shape our development as a species, one of the things we have to understand is that our nervous system builds up in layers," he says. "Maybe a little bit like an onion. You can't get rid of the original archaic layers of the central nervous system."[25]

He continues: "Those parts of the brain have evolved very gradually over millions of years in mammals, then in primates, and finally, in humans. Unfortunately, although we try our best to be rational and to weigh the pros and cons of decision making and to project into the future, we cannot obliterate the fundamental platform, which is our emotional brain."

Our emotional brain remains our freeze, fight, or flight stimulator. It's where the sensationalized melodramas come to life. Destructive emotions that live deep within us—like anger, revenge, and fear—are speculated here. Constructive positive emotions reside here, too, though it's usually those calamitous negative emotions that get our hearts pounding in fear over a high-stress project at work. In other words, our head often gets the best of us. More frequently than we'd like to admit, the way we are wired doesn't do us any favors. When it is time to make big changes, our fight or flight instinct kicks in.

Since we're hardwired this way, we have to learn to deal with these complicated emotions the best we can. "We have to accept the limitations of our ancient heritage," Alp says. "Then we have to come up with strategies that help us handle bad emotions and fear."

This explains why, as a people, we are often a bit too skeptical.

With two decades under his belt at Qualcomm, recently retired Roger Martin was a major player at the San Diego-based chip-making behemoth, a business that procures most of its profits from its patent licensing business, which Martin partially oversaw. With 220-plus worldwide locations and a hearty $26 billion in annual revenue, it's tricky to fathom that an institution with 33,000 employees would be concerned about what its tomorrow looks like.

But Martin admits he was worried.

"When things are going well, everybody's doing well," Martin says. "When it starts to not go so well, the people who are saying, 'It could get worse,' are looked at as 'Stop saying that' and 'You're hurting morale.' The people who cry the sky is falling can be immediately written off as a troublemaker, a lunatic, or somebody who's not in the party line or loyal to the company."[26]

When you are as colossal as Qualcomm, it's often hard to wrap your head around a dramatically different reality than the one you're currently living. Qualcomm, which has been hit hard with a handful of heavy global antitrust battles, is also dealing with the realities of halting mobile sales.

"At Qualcomm, my committee generated some presentations where we raised awareness about some situations that could happen," Martin says. "People were like, 'Well, gee, I hope that doesn't happen, I don't think it's going to happen, a lot of things would have to go wrong for that to happen—but I don't think it's going to happen.' Now the meeting is over, and I have to go back to what I was doing before, which wasn't preparing for this outcome."

Martin admits this is maddening. "You see it happen over and over again with the large companies that didn't see change coming. Nokia didn't see the smartphone evolution coming. They were just so big they were in denial."

It can be quite unnerving when you have consistently generated big revenue doing things a certain way, but this way will no longer suffice in the future. Indeed, change is hard and almost insurmountable when you don't think you need to change. We must be willing to recognize the need for change, and instead of being afraid of it, we should embrace it, despite the stories our head is telling us.

Truth #3: What got you here won't keep you here

Qualcomm's Roger Martin also happens to be an aficionado of zombie movies. He draws a commonality between the fictitious zombie apocalypse and the factual business apocalypse.

"The premise of every zombie movie is that somehow, somewhere—and it's always very mysterious—somebody got infected first," he says. "And they started spreading that infection. In hindsight, if someone in the beginning would have just recognized that the zombie was dangerous and taken it seriously, they could have just quarantined it and killed it. You could have wiped out the infection, and it would be over. The problem is that nobody believes that the danger is as big as it is. Because we're conditioned to believe that the status quo is going to continue forever."

He adds: "Qualcomm's infection was people wanted to stop paying us. Somewhere in China there was a company that said, 'Hey, I don't want to pay Qualcomm anymore. This is costing too much money.'"

The infection that started with one company in China began to spread to other companies on other continents. What once could have been easily contained became harder to wrangle and control.

"People start to think, we're big enough and we can contain it," Martin says. "We recognize that there's a problem. We're not going to close our eyes, but we're going to contain it. Everybody who's involved in trying to resurrect what existed before, those people die. They become zombie food immediately."

Martin has harsh advice for anyone shooting for futuristic relevance. "You have to stop doing the thing that right now is making you a ton of money," he says. "You have to start shifting, and that puts the current income stream at risk."

Change can be quite expensive and difficult, and it doesn't help that there's no guarantee what you do next will work. However, not changing isn't going to help you prepare or evolve for a drastically different tomorrow. Once you've made your way to the top, you must always be looking at ways to evolve your company to stay relevant and in demand.

Truth #4: You need time, but you don't have time

So this is where we are: Externally, your business is feeling the pressures of more competition and less control. Internally, your employees are wired to be a bit too self-serving, proud, or skeptical. Combine it all together, and you find yourself and your company stuck. This stasis means you can't change at the rate you need to.

Indecisiveness and uncertainty lead to slow decision making, and this can be your kryptonite: You must be urgent in addressing the changes that your company needs.

The most lucrative currency in the world is time. If we could go to Congress and fight for an eighth day of the week so that we could have more time, perhaps that would help. Since we can't, let's address the two major themes when it comes to corporate clock management.

We'll call them *turnaround time* and *turnover time*.

When it comes to turnaround time, or the time it takes to implement change within your organization, we must consider that we are living in a fast-paced business world that will only continue to get faster. This rapid world proves that the digital revolution is real and the requirement to make decisions quickly is here to stay. Unfortunately, when it comes to effectively managing time, we as a people are experts in slowing ourselves down. The speed to the right decision in business is often slowed because of the stresses that come from internal team dynamics. And where exactly does that stress come from? Deadlines and speculation.

Deadlines are realities of the job and leading the charge when it comes to stress buildup. Since we've already covered how our central nervous system reacts to pressure, we won't spend much time addressing the stress that comes from demanding deadlines; outside of when you have a deadline and you're not in alignment with your team. This often creates more work and more stress. Once you start to speculate, especially if you think you're on the path to missing one of these deadlines, your mind starts to focus on the wrong things. Add it all up, and we see how internal discord and time loss come to fruition. Which brings us to too little speed.

Nothing slows a team down like lack of trust, lack of empowerment, and lack of process. Lack of ability may also be on the list but most companies are decent at vetting employees.

Out of these four, it's lack of trust and lack of empowerment that get us into trouble. When you don't trust your players to do the job—when you get in their way while they are trying to produce—it slows the project down. Deciding when to step in, if at all, is naturally frustrating for any manager because you aspire to get the job done right the first time around. Usually your reputational currency depends on it! But the pressure that builds up in the manger can often be felt tenfold by the same team you're trusting to fulfill the project. Nobody's looking to work for a micromanager. When your players aren't empowered to do the job, for many, it's time to start looking elsewhere. And we're now seeing this reflected in job turnover data.

When it comes to turnover time, or that rate at which we lose and must hire new employees, according to a Deloitte 2018 Millennial Survey, over 43 percent of Millennials expect to leave their job in the next two years. This is a tricky one because your job is to teach this generation the skills they need to be successful in the workplace. If the statistic stands, then you just spent a lot of time and money training them for their "what's next." In that same Deloitte study, according to the US Labor Department, the percentage of workers of any age leaving their jobs has reached the highest level in more than 16 years.[27]

A 2016 study released by Russell Reynolds Associates also showed a record high turnover rate at the chief marketing officer position.[28] Russell Reynolds, which tracked publicly disclosed marketing turnover and appointments from 2012 to 2016, also suggests that replacement hires are not coming from within the walls of the organization. Through the first two quarters of 2016, more than 60 percent of hires were external.

First, external hiring exposes your potential corporate ceiling, no matter how loyal you are, when you stay at a particular company. Second, since the hire is from outside the organization, the new employee will need time—which they quite often aren't granted— to get up to speed on the business and team they've inherited. This severely slows down turnaround time and, not surprisingly, leads to more turnover.

Staff walking out the door with copious amounts of company knowledge can be a serious hindrance. Legacy employees, who are often looked at as stodgy organizational drawbacks, are usually that same group that carries a wealth of institutional knowledge.

On the flip side, it's quite often these same legacy employees who resist change and tend to revert back to the way life has always been inside your organization.

"The thing that drives a lot of traditional companies is the fear of losing what you already have," former Airbnb chief marketing officer Jonathan Mildenhall says. "That means you grow incrementally; you put artificial constraints on imagination, creativity, and innovation— particularly around marketing."[29]

So what gives? How do you turn this protect-the-revenue-you-already-have conundrum on its head? What can we do right now to change the future revenue game from incremental growth to exponential growth?

It starts by setting a firm expectation with your bosses, your board, and your team regarding what you plan to accomplish in an allotted amount of time. But this can be difficult to achieve when you haven't built up mass credibility within the walls of your organization.

As Salvador Dali once said, "Intelligence without ambition is like a bird without wings."[30] The wings of change often take flight when a willing, courageous soul first begins to drive change by making space to create and innovate within a stagnant organization.

In other words, you still need to muster up the courage to create that experimental breathing room with your superiors and your employees.

But before you can be that bold leader who slays the corporate gauntlet, it's critical that we deconstruct the way society looks at the word *courage* today. You'll soon discover that what many people perceive courage to mean is a major part of the problem.

THE SIX COURAGE MYTHS

ACCORDING TO THE *New Oxford American Dictionary,* courage means "the ability to do something that frightens one."[1]

I don't know about you, but this certainly doesn't sound like something I'm open to. If you ask me to take a step forward to do something that frightens me, I'll most likely take a step back. I don't wake up in the morning excited about doing something that I'm scared of—and I can't imagine I'm alone here.

Here lies our first problem: Almost no one is up for voluntarily doing something that takes courage, because we associate it with fear.

In your mind, you likely have some broad idea of what *courage* means. But courage as a concept is wildly misunderstood. I believe you can't truly understand what courage *is* without first understanding what courage *isn't*.

THE SIX COURAGE MYTHS

- Myth #1: Courage describes other people.
- Myth #2: Courage is jumping out of a plane sans parachute.

- Myth #3: Courage is a risky solo journey.

- Myth #4: Courage is impulsive.

- Myth #5: Courage can't be taught.

- Myth #6: Courage doesn't have a role in your daily life.

Without examining these myths, we can see how and why the idea of courage is rejected in boardrooms and business conversations nationwide. But once we dissect these myths and realize what courage is not, it can help us better understand how to properly unlock courage in our corporations, giving us a competitive advantage many others wish they could obtain.

MYTH #1: COURAGE DESCRIBES OTHER PEOPLE

When we think of courage, we can't help but picture extraordinarily brave feats performed by those in the military, firefighters, astronauts, or police officers. We're amazed by their honor, service, and sacrifice and wowed by how they risk everything for a higher purpose. We see them properly exalted thanks to Hollywood and in newsworthy press clippings. We allow ourselves to escape our everyday lives for a little while and imagine what we would have done had we been in the same situation. When the movies or news segments are over, most of us return to our safe and regular routines. The idea of being able to tap into this type of immeasurable courage is foreign to most of us. We simply can't relate since we aren't putting our lives on the line, nor are we superheroes.

This form of bold behavior I call *extreme courage*.

Most of us see these brave men and women as the most courageous, but these staunch citizens usually don't see themselves in the same light. They see themselves as simply doing their jobs. When you live your life this way, you don't label yourself as courageous. Or it's possible that the valiant, deep down, do think they are courageous; they just don't admit it because it would make them sound boastful. I think it's hard for most people to describe themselves as courageous.

Coleman Herbert is a Hollywood television writer who has penned episodes for shows such as HBO's *Big Love* and Hulu's *The Path*. Herbert has to put himself and his ideas out there on a regular basis and does so in writers' rooms all over Hollywood. "The stakes are really high," he says. "I think of it like an athlete's career. You are never going to play for 30 years or even 20 years."[2]

About being courageous, he adds: "It's not something you say about yourself."

After all, there's a big difference between having courage and saying you have courage.

Where extreme courage brings to mind the most audacious, there's a second type of compassionate courage that's designed for a community open to improving its intimate selves. This kind of courage is for people who are inspired by motivational pep talks and you're-not-alone, feel-good stories. Courage expert and researcher Brené Brown has made the word wonderfully relevant and meaningful to a heartened community of people who look to overcome strife with the help of courage in their own lives. Brown is a bona fide guru who has nudged others to muster up the courage to face personal demons, from shame to struggle, head-on.

I call this *encouraged courage*.

Extreme courage and encouraged courage are the most radical and the most vulnerable types of courage, respectively.

Well, what kind of courage is there for the rest of us?

I realized there was a kind of courage that was missing: *employer courage*.

If extreme courage and encouraged courage don't quite fit, then employer courage may be the kind of courage that you need. It will teach you how and when to be courageous at work. It provides concrete instructions that, once learned, will help you and your coworkers make astute, bold decisions that will help improve your business.

Employer courage teaches you how to be courageous with your business. (There will be more on this in the back half of the book, which includes a step-by-step, how-to guide to build your **Central Courage System**®.)

MYTH #2: COURAGE IS JUMPING OUT OF A PLANE SANS PARACHUTE

Jill Avery is a senior lecturer and marketing professor at Harvard Business School. After an illustrious career steering powerful companies such as Gillette, Samuel Adams, AT&T, and Pepsi, the sagacious Avery remains one of the go-to authorities on brand management. She recognizes the negative connotation that comes with courage.

"In business, a world where strategy and analysis are valued, courage can be misconstrued as reckless or rash," she says. "Like it's foolhardiness."[3]

Domino's president Russell Weiner agrees. "Think about this sentence said with different inflections," he says. "'That took *courage*' versus '*That* took courage.' They're the same exact phrase, but the takeaway is extremely different."[4]

Or consider my own mother, for example. When she says, "*That* was courageous," what she really means is "That was stupid." There's a very thin line between what is perceived as genuinely courageous and what is seen as reckless.

"How do you figure out what is just stupid versus what is courageous?" asks Andrew Turner, a category brand leader at Amazon. "A lot of early stage venture capital guys are building great products, and they've got total faith their vision's going to work out, but they don't understand market segment or the customer need. So they end up just spinning."[5]

In this sense, courage often gets misinterpreted as lacking strategy. It leads many to equate courage with making careless decisions that aren't grounded in wisdom.

Courage does not mean stupidity. Courage is not a suicide mission. In fact, courage should always start with *knowledge*.

Let's consider a skydiver for a moment, as an example of what I mean here. Let's assume this person is a member of the Red Bull wingsuit skydiving team. Most people have a hard time understanding how this jumper in a wingsuit can take that unfathomable leap. For many of us, the word *crazy* may come to mind.

Not this skydiver. They've done their homework to make this jump. They've relentlessly studied the weather and recognized what atmospheric conditions need to be in place to be successful. They know what forecast could arise that would require them to cancel. They have practiced, visualized, and studied the lay of the land. They know precisely how long they plan to be in the air and have their landing spot pinpointed exactly to ensure success. The skydiver has thoughtfully strategized their jump for maximum success.

When it comes to vaulting out of the metaphorical airplane of business, Russell Weiner says, "To me, courage is jumping out of a plane with a parachute, and that parachute is the data that you collect in preparation. It's the people that you surround yourself with. It's the product that you are bringing to market. It's all of that."[6]

In business, courage is leaping with a plan. Yes, sometimes plans change in the air and, no, there is no guarantee of success. But it's inevitable that if you forever stay the course without a plan for the variables that will come your way, you will surely not be able to keep going. And the repercussions can be fatal.

The sooner you realize that courage is not an aimless leap but rather a calculated decision that starts with knowledge, the better prepared you can be for tomorrow.

MYTH #3: COURAGE IS A RISKY SOLO JOURNEY

When breaking down this myth, we need to properly audit all three components: *risk*, *solo*, and *journey*.

Let's start with the journey.

Courage is primarily a *how*, not a *what*.

Courage is how you respond to those stressful business moments. Calculated, audacious leaders know that courage is right there with them in the muck of a difficult decision helping them deliver innovative products or liberating messages. It's sending a press release in which you take a bold, unified position on a controversial topic like gender pay equality.

With courage, TripAdvisor took a stance against promoting and selling tickets to animal attractions.[7] It wasn't the actual act of marketing this point of view that was courageous but rather the six months of research that culminated in a decision that most certainly rubbed some people the wrong way. At the same time, TripAdvisor must have known it would also attract heaps of passionate new customers who will reward the company for standing up for something meaningful.

> Courage is about the journey, and the desired destination is delivering something unapologetically meaningful.

While I believe that courage is undoubtedly a journey, I don't perceive it to be as risky as we think, nor do I think it's something that we face on our own.

Yes, there will always be some level of uncertainty when it comes to making courageous decisions, but those decisions are a lot less risky when you are prepared.

Wharton business professor Adam Grant, the best-selling author of *Originals: How Non-Conformists Move the World,* believes that "the most successful originals are not the daredevils who leap before they look. They are the ones who reluctantly tiptoe to the edge of a cliff, calculate the rate of descent, triple-check their parachutes, and set up a safety net at the bottom just in case."[8]

As we'll examine in Chapter 5 ("Prioritize through Values"), when you know yourself completely, when you commit to what matters most to you, it's easier to make the right choice—which feels less risky. Risk becomes less important than doing what you think is right.

Is courage a journey you take alone? I am certain there's no *I* in courage for a reason. Courage is less a "*me* thing" and more a "*we* thing."

No one gets to where they need to be alone. When it comes to courage in business, there is no "do it yourself"; there is only "do it together." You need your team to be on board to be successfully bold in business.

Sure, you definitely start on this journey alone because you have to opt in. There has to be a personal commitment. Once you willingly commit, you need to make sure you have a solid foundation and surround yourself with a loyal support system that will help you get through whatever strife comes your way.

This book is a prime example—it exists because so many people gave me access to their time, minds, and stories. When I shared, people shared back. From every piece of knowledge gathered through interviews, case studies, books, and colleague commentary, my faith in this concept increased.

As I relied on more and more people, the risk to my reputation decreased as well. There's no way I could have pulled this off by myself. So, yes, I was courageous and bet on myself, and then I connected with others who willingly shared and contributed their point of view. When I made courage about the group (*We need to be courageous*), it became much easier to openly discuss, accept, and claim.

The business world is tough enough. Going it alone is unnecessary. Even when you're a sole practitioner, you can hire a business coach, put in place an advisory board, or create an internal committee to help you through the tough decisions and potential hardships. If you have a solid plan in place and a committed team to help you, your journey will be less risky, and you won't have to feel—or go it—alone.

MYTH #4: COURAGE IS IMPULSIVE

We are all familiar with Hollywood blockbuster action movies. Often, the movie's main character gets in a predicament where they either need to be rescued or, like a hero, must swoop in, risking their own life and limb to save the day.

These edge-of-your-seat moments make great movie scenes. Unfortunately, many people misinterpret these off-the-cuff, gut decisions as courage.

This fictitious cinematic scenario—which may have been based on a true story—is anything but the truth. Back here in the real world, this kind of rash decision making comes off as reactive and lacking strategy. It's one of the reasons courage as a business value is rejected. Words like *fearless, brave, bullish,* and *courage* often get discounted in the workplace because they seem to not be anchored in a deliberate master plan. These words suffer the consequences of being considered impulsive, which leads many to avoid them.

This reminds me of Malcolm Gladwell's "10,000-hour rule"[9] unveiled in his well-known book *Outliers: The Story of Success.* If you have expertly built up your craft over a succession of years, if you have put in 10,000 hours at your profession, you probably have the know-how and experience to respond to certain scenarios faster than other people.

With that level of expertise, you can make quicker, smarter instinctual decisions that may appear to others as too fast.

A little over a year ago, my neighborhood embarked on a night of glamping with some other families in our community. At dusk, with our camping tents set up in our quaint local park, we heard shrieks from a nearby swimming pool. A little girl had been pulled from the water but was not breathing. While most of us froze, one of the fathers, an off-duty firefighter, went full speed toward the melee at the pool. In a matter of a few seconds, the firefighter was doing what he knew how to do—he began resuscitating the little girl.

Was this impulsive? Of course not.

It was a learned, *ingrained instinct.* We must learn and implement the same kinds of instincts with our approach to business.

Kathleen Reardon, in a 2007 *Harvard Business Review* article, "Courage as a Skill," wrote, "Through interviews with more than 200 senior and midlevel managers who have acted courageously—whether on behalf of society, their companies, their colleagues or their own careers—I've learned that this kind of courage is rarely impulsive. In business, courageous action is really a special kind of calculated risk taking."[10]

Back when I played high school baseball, we would practice as a team for two hours a day, four days a week. In practice, over and over again, we learned exactly what we needed to do on the field, *before* the ball ever left our pitcher's hand. If I was playing center field, and there was one out with a runner on first base, I knew if the ball was hit in front of me on the ground, I was throwing the ball to third base. If the ball was hit at me in the air, my job was to get that ball to second base as fast as possible.

To a spectator, this may have *looked* impulsive. My teammates and I knew different. We knew, with all that constant repetition, we were prepared to make seemingly fast decisions where ingrained instinct took over. This instinct came from experience, not from a gut impulse made on a hunch. It was something we trained and practiced for. Ultimately, it was something learned.

MYTH #5: COURAGE CAN'T BE TAUGHT

Though a great deal of information may be out there on courage, when it came time to find books that studied *business* courage, pickings were slim. Nor could I find a single course in a college curriculum on the topic. Though there are many classes on entrepreneurship and leadership, I didn't discover a single graduate degree program teaching "courageship" at the collegiate level.

Perhaps we don't prepare to be courageous because we perceive it to be innate. Or perhaps we disregard courage because we believe it can't be taught.

Giant Leap Consulting CEO Bill Treasurer sees it differently. "Contrary to popular belief, courage is a teachable and learnable skill, and most everyone has the capacity to be courageous," he says.[11]

Business courage is something we can grow like a muscle. We can begin to rehearse it in our everyday work lives. We can create a process that helps us practice courage.

Navy SEAL Jeff Boss equates it to the special operations practice of stress inoculation. "The more exposure you have to stress, the more your stress threshold increases," he says. "That's really the line of thinking behind our training. Our training is more stressful than anything else, which increases our capacity to deal with stress. To run a parallel line, courage, I would say, falls into that same category."[12]

Courage is not an inherent trait; it can be learned with practice. With repeated practice, anyone can achieve a state of courage. Routine makes it a habit. The more you train, the more you strengthen and stretch that skill.

Anything that we desire to be good at, we practice. Kids practice for music recitals. The great Michael Phelps practices to swim at the Olympics. The amount of time Phelps spends staring at that black straight line at the bottom of a pool is astronomical—repetition.

Unlike sports, every day in business is game day. Perhaps we don't make the time to practice business courage because, as we already discovered, time is always of the essence. But as we discussed in Chapter 1, we need to learn how to make calculated courageous moves to evolve our businesses.

Once you are aware that courage can be taught, you must take this information and choose wisely when to tap into its potential.

As Reardon wrote, "Courage is not about squandering political capital on low-priority issues. People who become good leaders have a greater-than-average willingness to make bold moves, but they strengthen their chances of success—and avoid career suicide—through careful deliberation and preparation."[13]

MYTH #6: COURAGE DOESN'T HAVE A ROLE IN YOUR DAILY LIFE

Think about something you did today that was unflinching and took courage. If you're like most, you either have to force an answer or you'd prefer to pass on this question.

Now think back to the last thing you did that was truly courageous. Naturally, it's easier when you step back and ponder the past and think about those bold moments in your life.

When we reminisce about the handful of courageous moves we've made in our lives, we can't help but nostalgically recall those few but daring leaps of faith. Maybe you moved to a new city where you knew virtually no one. Maybe you took on a cutting-edge job that required a skill set that was outside your comfort zone. Maybe you didn't accept a job offer until they agreed to match your salary counter.

Looking back, these were some big but scarce moments where you truly felt alive.

Because we don't partake in many courageous feats and don't perceive courage to have a role in the workplace, we don't believe courage has a place in our daily lives.

Jay Coen Gilbert, who cofounded shoe giant AND 1, admits that courage as a business concept only bubbles to the surface for him when he's prompted.

"Courage is just outside the core focus area," he says. "It's just outside the aperture. Once you tweak the lens and hone in on that out of focus thing, you realize, oh, that is totally relevant."[14]

There's a big difference between participating in a moment that, unbeknownst to you, is an act of courage versus having the ability to spot a brave opportunity when it presents itself. Most of us aren't able to detect these precious occasions. One of the goals of this book is to equip you with the tools you need to recognize those instances in life, as they're happening in real time, where you *should* boldly summon courage.

Training yourself and your teams to pinpoint those calculated moments where you override your nerves is key. The irony, of course, is that many of our most bullish servicemen conjecture that courage isn't at the core of who they are.

"I don't see anything that I've done as courageous," says Boss, the Navy SEAL. "I see it as a byproduct of the purpose I've pursued. It's the byproduct of going through my training."[15]

My friend Mike Rubino, a retired New York City firefighter, hung up his gear in 2009. Of his time with FDNY, he says, "We don't feel like heroes in the least bit. We are just carrying out our calling to protect in ways that others cannot, with a sense of duty, without hesitation."[16]

Those who have courage don't see themselves as courageous, and those who don't have courage misunderstand the definition as something wildly unattainable or not for them.

How did this happen?

Is it because of the six Courage Myths?

Resoundingly, no.

If the current working definition of courage is "doing something that frightens you," then it's time to boldly take a stab at redefining the word for the greater good of us all.

COURAGEOUSLY
REDEFINING COURAGE

IS IT CONCEIVABLE to make something that's scary *less* terrifying? Can we create a mechanism that takes the risk out of taking risks? Are we capable of crafting a formula that transforms making a courageous decision into a seemingly regular one?

I suppose it's courageous in and of itself to rework the definition into something more palatable—to give *courage* a new-and-improved, friendlier facelift. Maybe that way, more people will see that courage isn't just for heroes. With proper training, almost anyone willing can recognize, harness, and actualize courage in their everyday lives—and, subsequently, in their businesses.

Greek philosopher Aristotle considered courage to be the very first virtue because it makes all other virtues possible.

To be courageous, there first must be a commitment to willingness. Researcher Brené Brown writes of resilient leaders in her book *Rising Strong*, "They have the ability and willingness to lean in to discomfort and vulnerability."[1]

You have to want to be better. And that's not always a walk in the park.

The previous chapter debunked some popular myths and showed us what courage *isn't*. Now let's take a close look at what courage *is*. Here are the three essential factors that make up courage:

1. Knowledge

2. Faith

3. Action

Knowledge, faith, and action are the matchstick, tinder, and wood that work together to form the fire that is courage. The sum of these parts—and it must include all of them—makes up courage.

Courage always starts with knowledge. Obtaining knowledge is the true differentiator between doing something careless and embarking on something boldly calculated. It surely will be easier for you to take a risk if you are educated on the topic you need to be courageous about.

Since you're never going to be able to gather all the available knowledge on a given topic, at some point you have to rely on that belief system of yours we'll call faith.

And once you build that faith, mixed in with just enough acquired knowledge, then it's time to do something about it. This is when you take action.

You need all three—knowledge, faith, and action—for real courage to be at play. Two out of three in any combination is not courageous. Here's why:

- Gathering knowledge, building faith, and then taking no action is paralysis. We've all been in situations where we knew what we needed to do but, for some unknown reason, didn't pull the trigger. "Courage comes to those who act, not to those who think, wait, and wonder," motivational maverick Grant Cardone says. "The only way to hone this trait is by taking action."[2]

- Having faith and then taking action without proper knowledge is reckless. We're back to jumping out of a plane without a parachute. Remember, courage always starts with obtaining wisdom. Maya Angelou reminds us to "do the best you can until you know better, then when you know better, do better."[3]

- Gathering knowledge then taking action without having faith is simply too safe. This is status quo. If you don't feel a bit of nervousness on the inside, in a world saturated with choice, it's not enough.

> Acquiring knowledge, building faith, and taking action is courage.

The more you grow your knowledge and the more you grow your faith, the more courageous an action you should take. It's almost like having an inside scoop on how a stock is going to perform. When knowledge, faith, and action are in place, and when intuition suggests they work together in harmony, invest!

Let's break these down one by one.

KNOWLEDGE

Knowledge isn't just power; knowledge is an asset. The more you know, the more confidence you will have. Think about it in terms of preparing for an interview. When you study up on the company to which you are applying, you feel like you can ace whatever questions get tossed your way.

This kind of knowledge-based confidence becomes your ally in the business world—it's the firepower that's right there by your side, helping you dissolve doubt and transform a cynic into an ally.

Unfortunately, people's brains are wired to contest something that might seem new or risky, but real knowledge breaks down that barrier. Knowledge, properly articulated, creates confidence in the eyes of anyone you are trying to bring along with you on the journey of courage. Your knowledge makes it easy for people to both commit and buy in to your ideas.

Knowledge is the clarity collected through education or experience

It's the data, facts, and information that you absorb, allowing you to comprehend, understand, and grasp command of a topic or skill.

Access to knowledge by way of information has never been easier. The data that the Internet provides continues to expand at an astounding rate. With the click of a button, thanks to Google or Wikipedia, you can learn just about anything; all readily available on your mobile phone. And this is just the common person who doesn't have access to market-research-sized budgets.

Experiments are another way to acquire knowledge. Many office experiments end up being perceived as failures when they are anything but. These less-than-perfect experiences gathered over a period of time help us shape how we approach the next, new experiment. Stumbling into a failure is a big part of gaining knowledge.

We learn from these moments and we do our very best to not repeat history. Sir Richard Branson inked in his book that "you learn by doing, and by falling over, and it's because you fall over that you learn to save yourself from falling over."[4]

Mike Pearson, Google's ever-so-friendly director of business development and partnerships, has worked at the tech giant for over a decade. Pearson recalls how, after graduating from Harvard Business School, he was trying to decide between working at two companies. He wanted to work at a place that would provide a larger opportunity for innovation. Google offered an openness to try new things. With trying new things comes failure. The other company, he felt, was not as willing to take these kinds of risks.

Pearson spoke candidly about Google's internal quarterly performance evaluation and how it's nearly impossible to check all the boxes on a review. If you have checked all the boxes, you didn't fail enough and, ultimately, weren't stretching your potential on what is possible.[5]

Failures aren't looked at as mere failures at Google. The company plans for them, pivots off of them, and then—using this newfound knowledge—tries again. Google must take the data it learns from these failures and interpret its meaning to move forward.

This brings us to a question: Is data knowledge? Is it a means to achieving knowledge? The truth is that data and information are nothing without insight.

Erin Littrell is a digital marketer with an MBA from Wharton. "A lot of times I feel like we're marketers talking to marketers and pushing the message that we want or think should be meaningful to consumers without unpacking what is actually meaningful," she says. "The only way to do that is through data and insights."[6]

When harnessed properly, data can help take the guesswork out of many decisions, but the question remains whether the right data is being utilized and at what cost. Cost in this context is not what it takes in the short term to run a study but rather the long-term cost to your brand for making decisions based purely off data.

Data is not insight. Data is not knowledge; it is nothing without big thinkers who can take the data and make it useful.

"We are drowning in information, while starving for wisdom," biologist E. O. Wilson says. "The world henceforth will be run by synthesizers, people able to put together the right information at the right time, think critically about it, and make important choices wisely."[7]

Greg Kline, the head of market intelligence at a leading global research organization, has made a career excelling in the data comprehension arena. Kline agrees that we're only as good as the choices we make off the data we are provided with.

"There have been many times when I've had to walk into a room of experts who traveled in from around the world, and I had to tell them the program they believed was well orchestrated from data was, in fact, not what their clients wanted," Kline says. "It wasn't data alone that informed me of this. It was how my team had deciphered that exact same data but came to quite a different conclusion."[8]

Qualcomm's Roger Martin has had a similar experience. "Lots of people would come into my office and then show me charts and graphs, and they would think that their job was done," he says. "I would say, 'So what? What does that mean for us? What should we do if that is true? Now what do we do?' Data is just raw material. Insight and judgment create value."[9]

Data can be interpreted in different ways depending on the agenda of the interpreter. (You could make the case that I am pushing an agenda regarding *my* overall perception of data.) While I believe there is a clear role for data, it shouldn't supersede what matters most: being truly relevant and meaningful in a consumer's life.

Say you decided to go see an IMAX movie in 3-D starring Brad Pitt and Jennifer Lawrence. Thirty minutes in, you realize it's all sizzle and no substance. Data informed Hollywood that we like A-list celebrities and mind-bending special effects. However, with no compelling storyline, you've surmised this movie is a total waste of time and money.

This movie may open with a big box office weekend, but the truth always gets out, and it will show in the reviews.

Again, this is not to suggest that data doesn't have a useful role in our modern-day world. Data most often informs us whether we have the right message in play before we elaborate on that storyline. But you should have the courage to interpret what matters most from the data you are provided with and prioritize from there.

Google's Jason Spero knows just how valuable data can be. "The way my business customers think about data is that most people do try to see the data to justify a decision," he says. "They try to remove emotion. We work so hard to be data-driven. We look for proof points."[10]

As it relates to the idea of courageous decision making, Spero says, "I think, both for public companies and for everybody who's got a boss—whether it's shareholders, boards, or a CEO—when the numbers can't tell you fully to do it and there's a certain amount of leap, that is where you need to summon the courage."

When it comes to making complicated calls in business, you'll never have all the knowledge that you need. There will be missing pieces to the puzzle.

This is where our second lever of business courage kicks in to pick up the slack: faith.

FAITH

When we talk about faith, we're not talking about religion: We're talking about that little voice inside each of us better known as belief.

Reputation is often at stake when you choose to make a decision based on faith. Like the stock market, your reputation rises or falls with your successes and failures. This is why putting your neck on the line based on your belief in an idea without all the answers is hard.

Harvard Business School professor Jill Avery recognizes the importance of courage in business, from entrepreneurial start-ups to established and thriving businesses. "You see courage on display specifically with entrepreneurs who are putting themselves out there," she says. "They are journeying into an unknown new place with only the knowledge they've been able to collect and the conviction of making something new. You see marketers at big businesses making multimillion-dollar bets without all the answers."[11]

The mind-set of many in the business world doesn't help either. The cynics and the skeptics simply don't have, well, a lot of faith.

As Jocko Willink and Leif Babin wrote in *Extreme Ownership: How Navy SEALs Lead and Win*: "Leadership requires belief in the mission and unyielding perseverance to achieve victory, particularly when doubters question whether victory is even possible."[12]

Sometimes moving forward with faith is difficult. We often think about how successful we will be without considering how hard it will be to get there. Sometimes you have to commit to whatever hardships will come your way and confront that difficulty with the hope that it will lead to future triumph. This is especially taxing for start-up entrepreneurs who will be tested and critiqued by doubting coworkers, bosses, and even family members.

Mattress company Tuft & Needle's cofounder Daehee Park can relate. "When we were beginning, our parents and close friends were all questioning us," he says. "What are you doing with mattresses? They all assumed it was a side gig. What is it you're actually working on? It made us question why we were doing this."[13]

This was the moment where Park and cofounder JT Marino had enough knowledge and faith to hold firm. And because they did, they reached success. This reminds me of the famous quote credited to

German philosopher Arthur Schopenhauer stated in the nineteenth century, which still holds true today: "All truth passes through three stages. First, it is ridiculed. Second, it is violently opposed. Third, it is accepted as being self-evident."[14]

Park recalls: "The way we looked at it was we identified a clear problem [and] we saw a way to build something. Not just the mattress company, but a company that we wanted to work for, too. Our worst-case scenario was 'I guess we'll consult together and pay our bills that way.'"[15]

In their notorious 1980 book, *Positioning: The Battle for Your Mind*, Al Ries and Jack Trout wrote: "You must be willing to expose yourself to ridicule and controversy. You must be willing to go against the tide. You can't be first with a new idea or concept unless you are willing to stick your neck out. And take a lot of abuse. And bide your time until your time comes."[16]

This is why you need faith.

Faith powers you through when proof has yet to fully show itself

The road to your goal can be lonely. But evidence proves that if you work hard enough, you can eventually be a *MasterChef* winner. That's how it happened for "Latina on Fire" Claudia Sandoval.

Sandoval took down the season six cast of FOX's primetime hit TV show. Her life has been forever changed. "Knowing what I know now, I would have been way more courageous earlier on,"[17] Sandoval says, laughing.

When you have conviction and a strong understanding of what you want, though, it makes it easier to stay the course.

I know her story firsthand because the spicy Sandoval was interviewing to try to make it on the show while working for me at my previous creative agency i.d.e.a.

"I was happy at my job," she says. "I liked my team, but I wasn't able to use all of my strengths. I wanted to move on because I thought it was an opportunity to pursue something I always joked I could do better than all other contestants on the show before."

There were some friends and family who nudged her to try out, as well as some key family members who were unknowingly working against her. It truly was a test of her faith.

"My family was hesitant," she says. "My parents had spent 17 years in the food and beverage industry. They assumed that I had no idea what I was getting myself into. My mother didn't think leaving my job was smart. I was putting everything on the line leaving for Los Angeles with no understanding of how long I would be leaving for, but I had to try. It was my only chance at doing something I felt I was born to do."

Her parents were her metaphorical board of directors; they were constantly concerned about what she was risking. Like most boards that aren't involved in the day-to-day, they often don't have all the information regarding what's really going on. Nor do they have the time to truly grasp everything you are setting out to achieve. Their lofty position often hinders their point of view.

Having faith fuels our inner fire to combat our fears. Once Sandoval took the necessary action to commit to *MasterChef*, she added more than a dash of knowledge to her strong foundation of faith.

"When I found out I had made it, I had about a month to go before I left for Los Angeles," she says. "I reached out to a chef who let me borrow his *Culinary Arts Institute Encyclopedic Cookbook*. I knew I had to learn as much as I could about traditional techniques. The book was 1,400 pages, and I read it about three times between the time that I got it until the night before the finale. I never stopped studying. I wanted to learn as much as I could. When I had practice time, I worked my way through techniques and recipes I wasn't familiar with, but that I could make my own."

We already know this led to a victory.

"I surpassed even my own expectations by having just a bit of faith that I was destined to do this," Sandoval says. "I was so afraid to leap forward for something that I knew I was very much capable of doing. I needed to have faith in myself and in my ability to make it happen."

As faith sprouts, so should belief.

The more you believe, the more likely you can effectively pull the third and final lever of courage: action.

ACTION

As Aesop allegedly murmured, "After all is said and done, more is said than done."[18]

Inertia is the enemy. All the knowing and believing in the world is nothing if you don't leap. How many people or businesses know deep down what they need to do, but don't act on it?

Take, for instance, the goal of living a healthy lifestyle. If you ask a hundred people of all shapes, genders, and sizes how to lose weight, you'll likely get a similar answer from all of them—that it's a mix of diet and exercise. We all *know* how to lose weight. Yet we aren't disciplined enough to create and stick with an action plan. That's because the actual *doing* is hard. That's the difference between knowing and acting.

Courage is the act of doing even when there's resistance or fear.

That nagging ball of inner tension is why it's so hard sometimes to take action.

Staying frozen is your natural enemy. Being passive, doing nothing, or remaining stagnant is the worst thing you can do (or not do). Avoiding paralysis is key.

Of course, this is easier said than done. Many of us have been in heated internal meetings where we've battled back and forth on a topic only to be unable to reach a consensus. Instead, the team would spin like a top, coming to no actionable decision, and the meeting would disperse with no real movement on the issue.

So how do you overcome this lack of action?

Let's flash back to the early twentieth century and look to 1600 Pennsylvania Avenue for guidance.

Only the heaviest, most consequential and important decisions get elevated to the White House. President Teddy Roosevelt knew that if a complex problem that risked dividing the nation landed on his desk, he needed to deliver. Roosevelt once said, "In any moment of decision, the best thing you can do is the right thing, the next best thing is the wrong thing, and the worst thing you can do is nothing."[19]

Quite often, one step in the wrong direction is a step in the right direction—simply because you took that step. Once you make a recommendation, you have to move your team to accept that recommendation.

Only when you move on that decision will you enter the realm of action. Learn from that action. Formulate your intelligence based on that action. Then continue forward with urgency.

Speed plays today more than ever.

Burke Raine, a snack guy, knows a lot about his category, his competition, and making quick decisions. With a decade of salt, sweet, and savory experience, Raine recently left Hostess Brands to become the vice president and general manager of the snacks business at Conagra Brands. "I think we act fast and then, on certain things, we act really fast," Raine says. "That's just the nature of competition today. Everybody is upping their game. Everybody's smart. Every company is in the grind right now to maintain their relevancy."[20]

Raine believes the key to hitting corporate Mach speed comes through trust among your peers. "I think trust inspires speed, so laying the foundation to have great relationships across the different groups and enterprises that make up a corporation is critical to moving forward," he says. "Your culture is what enables you to move quickly."

Specifically, Raine says social media is one spot where you can amp up the tempo.

"In today's electronic environment, you can't move fast enough," he says. "You can be pretty nimble in e-commerce and social media. We tend to think about it as a communication vehicle, but it's probably the best real-time insights platform that anybody's ever devised. You can get tremendous feedback very quickly."

One of the sole areas where Raine cautions us to slow down is what a brand chooses to police in its social media feeds.

"I think where courage in social media comes into play is with relinquishing control over the message that marketers have so tightly held on to for so many years," he says. "You have a responsibility to not abuse that control. If someone writes in and says, 'I don't like your Twinkie flavor,' you may be tempted to delete their post, but if you do, you're undermining their trust. It's an open forum. If you try to assert control over that forum, you lose credibility of it being that safe place where ideas are welcome, and you kill your social vibe."

Social media is a dialogue, not a monologue. It's a two-way street and marketers have to be at peace with the comments posted on the platform. Use those responses as data points to help inform the action plan you create for tomorrow.

As the famous Japanese proverb goes, "Vision without action is a dream. Action without vision is a nightmare"[21]

Evan Jones is the chief marketing officer of the American guitar manufacturer Fender, a company he describes as a 70-year-old start-up. Fender's handcrafted guitars have shared the largest stages with some of the most iconic rock stars of all time, including Jimi Hendrix, Eric Clapton, and Stevie Ray Vaughan.

"We know that for this company to evolve, it's going to have to embrace the way that music has changed, and the way that people experience, digest, and learn music," he says.[22]

Knowledge is one-third of the battle.

"What's changed is the fact that the guitar shops were in the malls and main pathways for average consumers 30 years ago," Jones says. "Now they're in second- and third-tier malls. That Millennial isn't looking to go there to buy."

Jones says they're smack in the middle of creating Fender 2.0.

"Our definition of innovation is changing," he says. "It's not enough to iterate on a Fender Stratocaster body. We're transitioning what essentially is an endemic legacy business of longtime brick-and-mortar retail into a much more digitally relevant business."

As the Fender team evolves to mirror the modern ways guitar players participate in the act of learning or playing music, Jones admits this is the scariest part of the journey. This is where faith comes to fruition.

"There's no playbook or road map for this out there that we can look at. The faith part is being open to gut checking your desire, the way that you gather information, and then the way you choose to act upon it. Data's going to give us part of it; it's not going to give us all of it."

This is Fender's version of action. "If you're willing to assume that the truth is out there, then your job is to go find it," Jones says. "If you're willing to put the consumer's desires ahead of a company decision, then you're always going to default to the right spot."

To achieve courage you must be knowledgeable, have faith, and take action. This new definition of *courage* leads us to our working definition of a *Courage Brand*:

> A Courage Brand willingly addresses its business fears by gathering enough knowledge, building faith, and taking swift action.

When senior management teams adopt this new approach to courage, they can evolve and transform their companies. This new definition is one you can rely on and turn to during real-time moments when you need it most.

Behind every thriving Courage Brand is a courageous group of internal believers who willingly commit to their belief system, even when it's hard, for the greater good of the company.

In almost every circumstance, these brave believers value the four principles of courage explored in the next chapter.

THE FOUR PRINCIPLES
OF COURAGE

YOUR NERVOUS TOES are dug firmly into the sand on the edge of an ocean. While you've spent decades swimming in the safe and clear confines of a pool, you're now seconds away from plunging for the very first time into the murky, deep blue. Without knowing how to swim in these conditions, you nervously wonder, *How will I respond?*

With one deep breath, you take the plunge.

In a blink, a version of survival mode kicks in as a pummeling of dark saltwater from all directions swallows you whole. As you fight a swelling undercurrent below, you simultaneously attempt to navigate continuous, crashing waves above. Naturally, you're focused solely on the largest task in front of you—*not* drowning. Paralysis isn't an option. Every iota of your body and mind is locked in on this new, unnerving, and frightening predicament. You keep pumping your arms and legs trying to power through this new unknown.

A moment later, you break out of the choppy roughness and emerge successfully on the other side of the waves into a beautiful, quiet calmness. Your panic has morphed into peacefulness. Under the sun, you enjoy a few blissful seconds of ocean serenity.

Elated now that you've arrived in personal unchartered waters, you think to yourself how you almost didn't jump in. You wonder what life would have been like if you stayed up there on that sandy beach.

Deep down, you would have regretted it.

As your swimming improves with every stroke, you look up and, to your surprise, you notice a man on a raft paddling your way.

You and this man make your way toward one another. When you meet, he pulls you up to safety where you admire an entirely new perspective above the deep blue ocean.

The man steering the raft points out a few others around the break of the beach where you had been before. There stand a handful of scared individuals who haven't mustered the courage to make the leap.

Perhaps missed by the man, you then point out a few others in the ocean who are swimming your way. Together, the two of you help a handful of willing swimmers up onto the raft with you to share this new perspective.

As raft mates, it helps to have committed team members who aren't afraid to leap into those murky, unknown waters with you.

If you're going to embark on a courageous business adventure or create a Courage Brand, consider what type of person you want on your raft with you. What collection of diverse skills do you hope they have that perhaps you don't? Will your raft mates have a hopeful, positive attitude? Are they strong communicators? What type of preparation will you and your floating troupe take part in before your journey?

These answers will become clear as we examine the four principles of competent and courageous decision making:

1. Talent

2. Team

3. Tenacity

4. Training

TALENT

It all starts with the talented people you recruit.

When your talent is truly top-notch, you can empower them with the ability to steer the raft. As Steve Jobs once said: "It doesn't make sense to hire smart people and then tell them what to do; we hire smart people, so they tell us what to do."[1]

What separates your very best people from the rest?

Their ability to consistently be counted on to get the job done.

What's the most beautiful thing about the most talented people?

They never think they are talented *enough*, so they keep pushing, working, and stretching themselves to be better. They have a constant desire to continue to grow their talents. They set a high bar for themselves, and they work hard until they reach that goal. They are driven, and they can be relied on to succeed time and time again.

Accomplished people are high achievers who exceed at skill and will. These adept team players want to surround themselves with other talented people. If we are, as motivational speaker Jim Rohn believed, the sum of the five people we spend the most time with, then how talented are you?[2]

Nothing is more frustrating to one of these star players than having to work with someone who slows them down.

Patty McCord, the former chief talent officer at Netflix, wrote, "The best thing you can do for employees—a perk better than foosball or free sushi—is hire only 'A' players to work alongside them. Excellent colleagues trump everything else."[3]

Or as Bill Gates noted in 1992: "Take away our 20 best people and I tell you that Microsoft would become an unimportant company."[4]

This means effective hiring is everything. It's what led Elon Musk to personally interview the first 1,000 Tesla employees. Musk understands the importance of slowing down to assess and hire the right people to include on his team. (We'll cover more on this topic in Chapter 6, "Rally Believers.")

The way to keep your skilled talent is not simply by surrounding them with other talent but by giving them meaningful projects that often need courageous decision making. Remember, for instance, Mike Pearson and his decision to work for Google. When he was deciding between two companies to work for, he chose the company that he perceived would present the greater of two challenges.

Not surprisingly, talented people have talented ideas. As Google's cofounder Larry Page says: "Good ideas are always crazy until they're not."[5]

Being able to go to bat and consistently get hits for your organization is what makes you valuable. To keep the baseball metaphor going, let's say you do your part and are now on base. Now, you need someone else to knock you home.

TEAM

Did you know diamonds and graphite are made up of the same stuff?

Both the cherished diamond and the less-appreciated, chalky graphite are made up of carbon atoms. Yet one is known for its extraordinary brightness, strength, and value, and the other is dull, black, and absorbent.

How can two substances composed of the exact same stuff be so different? The answer is how the carbon atoms are arranged.

A diamond's atoms are tightly bonded. It takes more time, heat, energy, and pressure to form diamonds—and as we all know, their glimmer is quite eye-catching.

The atoms of graphite consist of flat bonds. Some of these bonds are strong, but they are often working with weaker bonds. Graphite is more cooperative than diamonds, perhaps too cooperative. This means that some of the strong bonds try to make the most of the looser bonds. These weaker delocalized bonds tend to loosely slide and glide over one another—ultimately diminishing the potential of what could have been.

Remember, courage is a team sport. You want your team to be bonded by bright, strong, and valuable members. Having your senior leaders function like a desirable, transparent, and precious diamond is one way to make an admired, harmonious work culture. The structure, tightness, and rigid conviction exuded by a unified team can be the difference between success and failure.

Buddhist sage Thich Nhat Hanh wrote, "If we try to go to the ocean as a single drop of water, we will evaporate before we ever arrive. But if we go as a river, if we go as a community, we are sure to arrive at the ocean."[6]

What does it take to make the right team?

The dynamics of picking the right people for your team are complicated. They must possess the desired characteristics, and they must have the right fit.

The right people put the team first. They fit because they not only have undeniable talent, but they also have that "it takes a village" mindset—they are collaborative and cooperative. Navy SEAL Jeff Boss knows a thing or two about teamwork. Boss professes, "No one person is smarter than everyone else. Nothing gets done more effectively than when people work together. The team is everything. It's central to performance and results."[7]

Jeff Ragovin, who cofounded Buddy Media (later sold to Salesforce in 2012), recalls the critical importance when trying to get Buddy Media off the ground of finding the right people for his team. "We didn't necessarily get it right from the start," he says. "Some didn't make it. But when we found the right people, and the right chemistry, it was amazing to see something grow and flourish so beautifully."[8]

Sometimes the right people are those you've worked with at other companies along the way. Other times, it's buddies from business school or from growing up.

Jay Coen Gilbert and his two closest friends built up basketball brand AND 1, and after a 13-year run culminating at number two in the market, sold the company in 2005 for more than a quarter of a billion dollars. The three friends' next step was cofounding a nonprofit organization called B Lab, which serves a global movement of people using business as a force for good.

"For 23 years I have worked with my closest friends in two very different contexts, and neither of those businesses would have been successful if I had tried to do them on my own," Gilbert says. "I'd say more important than friends is just recognizing that business is a team sport. So the question is, who will make the best teammates?"[9]

He adds: "You want people who are more skilled than you but that you also trust implicitly, and it's even better if you've got love for each other."

Skills. Trust. Love.

Not all of us have the luxury of starting a business with our best friends, but when you harmoniously work with a diverse team of gifted experts who are on the same page, it's certainly easier to eliminate doubt.

Indeed, great people on great teams want to succeed together. Harry Truman put it best: "You can accomplish anything in life, provided that you do not mind who gets the credit."[10]

I recall when my advertising company pitched for the Eddie Bauer business for the second time in three years. The first time, we had left a strong enough impression that when the account came back up for review, they asked us if we would throw our hat back into the ring. When we accepted, we decided we wanted to capture our team "living their adventure," which remains the sentiment of the Eddie Bauer brand today.

Only catch?

We didn't want our pitch team to know, so we set up an elaborate plan.

Over the course of two weeks, we successfully convinced our team that they were heading to Los Angeles for a capabilities presentation with my cofounder Jon Bailey. Jon, who runs the relationships side of the business, had shared that the client was a friend of his and that no meetings or practice would be needed to win the account.

The morning of the faux pitch, Jon sent out an email to the group breaking the bad news: He had been up all night with food poisoning, and I would be taking over on his behalf. Up to this moment, from the team's vantage point, I was coming in completely dark, as I hadn't been included on a single email about this opportunity until this very morning.

The team was instructed to meet at my house on their way up to Los Angeles, and after they arrived, unbeknownst to them, hidden cameras captured their reactions to me being rather unimpressed with their presentation. With tension reaching its climax, I unveiled their next 24 hours. I did so by asking them to walk out the side door of my house, where I unveiled a souped-up Winnebago that was waiting for them.

One by one, each team member entered the motorhome to find personalized head-to-toe Eddie Bauer gear waiting for them. Moments later, with suits ditched and adventure garb on, off to a desert campground we went.

All of this was documented on camera by our production team—including the next 24 hours of us sharing stories and getting to know each other around a campfire away from our cell phones and laptops.

A few weeks later, we opened our pitch meeting with the video of our team getting tricked. Four minutes into our presentation and I felt genuinely confident we had won over the room.

Days later, I got the phone call we were hoping for: The client was beaming that we had gone to such lengths to show them how much we cared about their business. We were awarded the account right then. This was a complete team effort that utilized almost every department in our office. From production to PR, from client partnership to creative, we could not have pulled this off without all of us working together. Account won. Credit shared.

This brings us to the importance of team breadth. Something about that pitch team that helped us land the Eddie Bauer account was having team members with different and relevant strengths. Having a wide swath of diverse knowledge on the team truly made our ideas and therefore, our pitch, better.

Russell Wallach, president of media and sponsorship at Live Nation, recently realized a goal of team diversification and transformation. "Brands are getting more sophisticated," he says. "One of the things we felt we needed to do was truly bring more brand and agency experts onto our team to continue to help translate our business to brands. Now we go out to the marketplace with a real understanding of the challenges those brands are facing. Not just thinking about it from a purely musical standpoint, we are capable of helping them solve their biggest challenges at the brand level."[11]

That blend of different made all the difference.

And it was a form of courage for Wallach to hire people from outside the music sector. He admits the learning curve for them to understand the music business was *less* than he anticipated.

"I think it's because they start with an understanding of how a brand thinks or how an agency works. They are actually helping us simplify our business for how we approach brands."

Finally, the people joining the team should only come on board if the cultural shoe fits. If you personify yourself as more of a "wing-tip" or "loafer" person, you might want to think twice about joining a sneaker culture.

What often happens with great people who don't fit your culture is they leave bitter within the first year. Not only does your yearlong investment walk out the door, but these people can also damage your reputation by talking negatively about your business.

TENACITY

So here you are. You're with the right team members, on your competent, committed business raft full of talent. That diverse talent makes up a team with the right mind-set to conquer terrifying business uncertainties. This brings us to our third principle regarding how the team grittily takes on tomorrow's unknowns: *tenacity.*

Facebook chief operating officer Sheryl Sandberg inspiringly addressed the 2016 graduating seniors at the University of California, Berkeley. "It is the hard days—the times that challenge you to your very core—that will determine who you are," she told the crowd. "You will be defined not just by what you achieve, but by how you survive. You are not born with a fixed amount of resilience. Like a muscle, you can build it up, draw on it when you need it. In that process, you will figure out who you really are—and you just might become the very best version of yourself."[12]

Tenacity is persistence plus resilience.

It is the constant pursuit of truth, a sibling of curiosity and the antithesis of laziness. It draws upon willingness, commitment, and a healthy dose of determination to power through unforeseen obstacles on the quest for your desired outcome.

What's my personal life mantra? *I am patiently relentless.*

It took me three years to make my high school varsity soccer team. Four years to get into the creative department of one of the largest New York City advertising networks. Five years before I won my first true national client as an agency owner. Being patiently relentless is a commitment to the journey, and it sets an expectation of how long that journey will take.

There will be speed bumps along the way.

Though when you're ready for the speed bumps, it's better to face them with a team that shares your resilient, tenacious attitude.

Attitude certainly matters, and a dose of positive tenacity can go a long way.

Stone Brewing cofounder and executive chairman Greg Koch describes it as "having an unrealistic positive view on how the future will work out. Then, of course, we work to bring that to fruition."[13]

Having a positive attitude and working with others who share that characteristic also brings joy. Driving down the road less traveled with other enthusiastic journeyers inspires us to stay on track. Tapping into your faith and keeping a positive attitude can keep you and your team moving smoothly along.

IBM's Lou Gerstner wondered, "Who wants to work for a pessimist? Who wants to work for a manager who always sees the glass as half empty? Who wants to work for a manager who is always pointing out the weaknesses in your company or institution?"[14]

Truth be told, almost every decision made on the business battlefield is out of your control. Most of us don't have a say when it comes to picking our officemates. We don't get to make the call when our boss needs us to work a weekend. There's not much we can do when a client cancels a meeting or a coworker on a deadline takes a sick day.

One thing we can always control is our attitude. You get to decide every day how you show up, and good things usually happen when you show up with a good attitude.

Even if you fail, if you have tenacity, you can learn from those failures and turn them into positives. Over time, if you keep trying and learning and continuing on your path, you will succeed. It wasn't until he was in his 60s that Colonel Sanders, after pitching his KFC secret recipe over 1,000 times, found a believer and an investor.[15]

Nothing comes easy when you are pursuing something new; just ask Elon Musk.

In Ashlee Vance's book *Elon Musk: Tesla, SpaceX, and the Quest for a Fantastic Future,* Antonio Gracias, who sits on the Tesla board, recalled Musk's even-keel tenacity during his most trying times. This included constant press ransacking, the demise of a marriage, and the loss of a child. "He has the ability to work harder and endure more stress than anyone I've ever met," Gracias said. "What he went through in 2008 would have broken anyone else. He didn't just survive. He kept working and stayed focused."[16]

Vance suggested this is Musk's competitive advantage: to limit the noise and outwork and out-persevere the competition. "Their decisions go bad," Vance wrote. "Elon gets hyper rational. He's still able to make very clear, long-term decisions. The harder it gets, the better he gets."[17]

Musk is a tenacious warrior. Warriors know nothing worthwhile comes easy. Warriors are not wavered by the pain. Warriors are committed to that long and winding journey. Most of all, warriors know, over time, they will get themselves to their desired victorious outcome.

Now imagine congregating multiple warriors whose values are aligned and are ready to battle together. Great teams show a resilient commitment to stay the course in pursuit of success, through thick and thin.

Again, tenacity is persistence plus resilience.

TRAINING

Warriors don't start out that way. They take the necessary time and steps to learn and transform into battle-ready soldiers. They do so by building their talent through hours and hours of rigorous practice.

Jeff Boss wanted to be a Navy SEAL because he wanted to do something different with his life—something exciting that allowed him to literally jump out of planes.

"If becoming a SEAL was possible, despite however many people failed the selection process, if it was possible then I could do it,"[18] he says.

Boss spent 13 years in the Navy. He had eight deployments, dealt with four parachute malfunctions, was shot twice, and lost way too many friends.

He talks regularly about team training as a SEAL—how each member strives to make themselves and their teammates better and how no person is more important than the team. His team trained as a unit and did everything in their power to contribute what they knew to help advance the entire team forward.

"The team that was deployed at the time would share their lessons learned," he says. "That would shape how we trained. That allowed us to stay on the cutting edge. It allowed us to be prepared for when we were overseas so that we could not ignite or activate that courage but employ it."

Navy SEALs meticulously train for missions over an extended period of time. Their training includes process, practice, and repetition for hours on end. A marathon runner also embarks on this same type of training. Long distance runners don't simply wake up one morning and conquer a marathon. There's regimented training. There's a reason 99 percent of marathon runners finish their races: It's because they are disciplined.

That discipline is a critical component of training for courage. So much so that when you ask somebody who has courageously mastered their training, it starts to feel less and less like courage.

CBS anchor Carlo Cecchetto is on the front line covering this country's most compelling stories. "The policemen and firefighters I talk to that are involved in those crazy situations, they don't think they're heroes," he says. "They don't think they're courageous. They're just doing what they thought they should do."[19]

The irony?

To outsiders, these feats are courageous. To the trained insider, the behavior has become second nature. Instead of having a fear of the unknown, these people have the familiarity of the known.

When training transforms into instinct, the idea of courage fades. Skilled teams that have been properly trained don't believe that they're courageous. The training has fully taken over, and muscle memory is at work.

This isn't simply describing people who willingly took on the challenge of courageous training. It also describes those who weren't expecting to opt in on courage.

Patricia Chapin-Bayley is head of enterprise solutions at Toluna, a market research and insights company. When she was a university student, she took a job with one of the largest banks in Toronto. With little to no experience, Chapin-Bayley was given a significant amount of training to handle the stresses that could come with the job of bank teller.

"We all know bank robberies happen, but I didn't even consider it a real possibility," she says, "The understanding of this risk and my fear forced me to pay very careful attention to the robbery training module. It repeated robbery scenarios again and again, and we were shown videos of simulated robberies with the correct way to respond—the bank teller was shown acting out the very steps we were being trained on."[20]

Thanks to entrenched muscle memory, Chapin-Bayley knew the robbery training methodology by heart. A year later, she was forced to put this process to work.

"No one was paying attention to this man and our transaction," she says. "He spoke to me quietly and said, 'I'm here to rob the bank. This is a robbery; don't make it a homicide.' He lifted his jacket to show me the gun he had concealed."

Chapin-Bayley switched into autopilot. She spoke to the man calmly and steadily. She followed all the learned protocols, which kept her colleagues safe and minimized the loss to the bank.

It wasn't until the robber walked out of the bank that Chapin-Bayley broke down. But it was the extensive training that enabled her to handle the situation with minimal thought. "I didn't feel I was courageous at the time—I was just doing what I was trained to do and what was expected of me," she says.

For many in business, the lack of rigorous workplace training is a big problem. We are not good at providing our employees with the proper tools and tips they need to be effective in the office. Either the training time is too short, or the programming is not as potent or repetitive as it needs to be.

Verne Harnish addresses this in his book *Scaling Up*. "In sports, the team gets to practice 90 percent of the time and perform 10 percent," he wrote. "In business, it's the opposite: We're lucky if we get 10 percent of the time to practice through executive training and development."[21]

I had an old soccer coach who preached, "Practice doesn't make perfect. *Perfect* practice makes perfect." Not only do you need training, but you also need relevant training at game speed that enables you to do your job in real time.

Train according to how you want to perform. What we're really talking about here is preparation. To train is to prepare.

Former basketball coach Bobby Knight says, "The key is not the will to win . . . everybody has that. It is the will to prepare to win that is important."[22]

In business, being prepared helps keep us away from our instinctive freeze, fight, or flight reactions to tough situations. Some experts have suggested it's 95 percent freeze or flight and only 5 percent fight.[23] We need training to override the way we're wired. The psychological speed bump we must often cope with is our overly protective central nervous system, and we've already covered how that doesn't do anything to help.

We are all equipped with our sympathetic and parasympathetic nervous systems. The sympathetic up-regulates (or activates our fight or flight responses) while the parasympathetic, from a physiological sense, helps down-regulate our bodies (slows our heart rate and conserves energy). The system works together, in tandem, to help power our bodies when we need that extra push away from danger. It also tempers our heart rate or breathing during mega stressful situations.

Emily Cox-Martin is an assistant professor and practicing clinical psychologist at the University of Colorado Anschutz Medical Campus. An expert on how the brain and body work together, she understands how our central nervous system means well but often gets in the way.

"In terms of what our central nervous system used to do for us evolutionarily, imagine you are hunting for food and there is a bear," Cox-Martin says. "You love these blueberries, that bear also loves these blueberries, and he wants you to get away from the blueberry bush. The sympathetic [nervous system] kicks in, and it takes all the blood away from your heart and pumps it toward your large extremities—like your large muscle groups and your powerful quads so you can run. It releases cortisol into your body from your adrenal glands. All the chemical signals that you need to be able to breathe faster release oxygen in a certain way so that your muscles can mobilize rapidly. Once the fear has subsided, your parasympathetic [nervous system] begins to take over saying, 'Hey let's settle down, let's calm down. We're okay now. We're back in our cave. We've got our berries.'"[24]

Cox-Martin says that while the back-and-forth process of our central nervous system was optimal in the caveman days, the way this system affects us in modern times is antiquated.

Our central nervous system used to save our lives; now, even when we're facing minor threats not involving grizzlies, our nervous systems aren't equipped to detect a difference. Our heart begins to pound, our breathing is affected, and it's increasingly more difficult for us to function. It works against us in the office and can lead to paralysis, team dysfunction, and even costly sick days that halt productivity.

Thanks to technology, we can keep up with everything that goes into our bodies. Our phones can help us count calories. Our computers can send alerts to remind us when to take life-saving medicine. But the way we are wired still holds us back.

Our smart watches may be able to perfectly pinpoint how many beats per minute our heart races, but it provides no compelling data as to why your heart is trying to escape your chest. So how do we cope when our freeze, fight, or flight response kicks in?

John Assaraf, a key contributor to the book *The Secret*, is the founder and CEO of NeuroGym. Assaraf, who describes his company as a mental gym for your brain, believes that "it's all about helping people recognize the mental and emotional obstacles that are holding them back and teaching them ways to train their brain to release them to get to the next level."[25]

An accomplished serial entrepreneur, even Assaraf deals with the realities of his central nervous system. "Every time I want to achieve more, the insecurities come up. Am I smart enough? Am I good enough? Am I to that level? I think I could do that, but then there's a little voice that goes 'What if you don't?'"

> The good news for all of us is that we have the capacity to calm that little voice inside our heads. We can train ourselves and learn how to be courageous.

You don't need Wi-Fi to access courage. Courage doesn't need to be plugged into a wall nor is there an app you can download to find it.

Training the brain is the answer.

We can overcome the realities of our central nervous system.

We can create processes that, over time, help us repeatedly make courageous decisions in our rapidly changing world. We can prepare for and practice courage. When we practice, we make a habit. When we make a habit, we create routine.

Enough talk.

It's time for action.

PART

2

The Central Courage System

"The reason so many effective solutions take forever
to get implemented is that the fear of change is
greater than the cost of sticking with what you've got.
In other words, people wait until they have a heart
attack or get diabetes before they go on a diet."[1]
—Seth Godin

THE BEST ORGANIZATIONS know what they stand for inside and out. They work hard to be aligned in their values from the top down. They identify and address problems head-on. They face business fears with a truthful purpose the entire organization can rally behind. Finally, they take action, executing new relevant products, services, or messages that convince others to buy in, believe, and share.

Ultimately, they transform themselves into a Courage Brand.

The path to morphing into a Courage Brand isn't easy. If it were easy, everyone would become one. Lecturing author Jim Collins reminds us,

"It's what you do before the storm that most determines how well you'll do when the storm comes."[2]

Many of us take self-defense classes so we're equipped to protect ourselves or our families, just in case, down the line. Consider learning how to become a Courage Brand as business self-defense.

Let the **break-glass-*before*-emergency** training begin.

How do we change "There's no time like the present" to "There's no time *but* the present"? How do we inject a sense of urgency into a sensible plan? The way to do so is to build your skills before you actually need them and before the emergency strikes.

We all have a central nervous system. Soon you will learn how to create a Central Courage System for your company. The Central Courage System combats the realities of the skeptical freeze or flight response that we are wired with. Once the training is fulfilled, your Central Courage System will help you make quick, calculated, and courageous decisions with your employees.

The Central Courage System is a process that your team can repeatedly turn to for guidance. Once it has been established and implemented, you can lead with your system's values, purpose, and point of view.

Thomas Purcell, the oncology system director at the University of Colorado Hospital health system, reminds us that those who are committed to fighting cancer willingly follow a disciplined regimen.

"People need to know that there's a program," he says. "They need to buy in to that program and ultimately go through that program. In order to achieve, you must believe."[3]

In business, having a Central Courage System is that program.

When you follow the training, making courageous decisions becomes ingrained instinct not spontaneous impulse. Speed is key. The Central Courage System teaches us how to make bold, swift decisions.

It's vital that we focus on the *system* of the Central Courage

System—a high-functioning systematic process you can turn to when you need it most.

What we are going up against is daunting. As you recall, you urgently need a Central Courage System for four reasons:

1. Companies are perishing at an alarming rate.

2. We are afraid of change.

3. What got you here won't keep you here.

4. You need time, but you don't have time.

Most people wait for that code-red moment before they begin to react. Many hope it never comes and don't think about potential turmoil until it's too late. So it should come as no surprise that building your Central Courage System comes at a cost, which can be quantified as a five-step process, easily summed up as P.R.I.C.E:

Prioritize. Rally. Identify. Commit. Execute.

- **Prioritize** through values
- **Rally** Believers
- **Identify** fears
- **Commit** to a purpose
- **Execute** your action

> P.R.I.C.E. is the courage instructional manual that can help shape your company's Central Courage System.

Whether you're a start-up from Silicon Valley or a legacy brand, the path to building your Central Courage System is the same. Whether you're aspiring to start a new company, turn a business around, or are in the process of making a courageous personal brand decision, my hope is that you will conquer your largest business fears by following the training described in the next five chapters.

It all starts with the first, and most important, overlooked step of them all: **prioritize through values.**

PRIORITIZE
THROUGH VALUES

IMAGINE YOU'VE JUST enlisted in the Army with little knowledge of what's to come. As you ink your final paperwork, the recruiting officer reveals your newfound destination of Fort Knox, Kentucky. He briefly enlightens you about your very near future: 16 weeks of basic training and eight mission-focused drill sergeants who are responsible for transforming you and your fellow recruits from regular civilians into expert soldiers.

This process, as you can imagine, is fixed and has been for quite some time. It's 17 concentrated hours a day of detail-oriented programming. The training gets progressively more intense as you move from the first month to the fourth month.

The first 30 days is a concentrated dose of exercise, clockwork precision, and military protocol. This includes a daily 90-minute early bird special of endless push-ups and running in cadence with a drill sergeant. It's classroom work, like learning the military rank structure and sponging up the history of the Army. It's practicing in the field, remembering formations, and properly learning how to communicate with superiors. Finally, it's countless maddening military marching exercises.

There's one other wildly fascinating lesson that you as a soon-to-be soldier partake of during basic training. You must learn the Army's seven core values, summed up in one tidy, easy-to-remember acronym: LDRSHIP.

LDRSHIP STANDS FOR:

- Loyalty
- Duty
- Respect
- Selfless Service
- Honor
- Integrity
- Personal Courage

Along with getting into optimum shape, asking each basic trainee to adopt these seven core values is one of the Army's top priorities. A certain percentage of new recruits who roll through the doors of the Army show up directionless, and these values help them understand where they need to go.

These shared values have been visibly plastered all over the grounds at basic training facilities. They act as meaningful reminders, helping each soldier know *how* they should behave, even when there is no longer a superior barking at them telling them exactly what they need to do. After running the exercises of basic training, many can now prioritize what's worthy of their attention.

LDRSHIP isn't just some check-the-box acronym painted on a few Army basic training barricades. Rather, the Army is committed to making its values matter to all of its service men and women, in all facets of their lives. Each of these seven words holds deep meaning, and each has been thoughtfully chosen to create the desired behavior of the armed forces.

One of the boots on the ground soldiers we interviewed for this book stated, "Once I started using the LDRSHIP acronym in my everyday life and not just in my Army life, it fundamentally changed who I was at my core," he says. "They will always stay with me for the rest of my life. I still use them to this day."

This values philosophy isn't something that should be hoarded by our military; it's important for any modern-day business, being, or brand. When you lead through your company's values, when they are relevant and ingrained in your people, your teams earn permission to make fast, calculated, courageous decisions. And they can do so without feeling like they are wavering from your business's belief system.

> How will you know when to take a stand if you
> don't know what you truly stand for?

KNOW YOUR VALUES

The future is unknown, unforgiving, and ever-changing. It's difficult for many of us to navigate this uncertainty, stay true to our corporate culture, and evolve our business properly forward.

Many businesspeople talk about their search for their company's North Star. Better defined, many leadership teams are looking out into the yonder for some sort of futuristic, metaphorical lighthouse to run toward. Most people think this lighthouse is somewhere in the distance, but I believe the lighthouse is right beside you—always there for you to turn to and rely on. That lighthouse is your distinguished, distinct core values.

Unfortunately, many companies don't get this right. Employees disregard existing company core values as irrelevant. This happens for one of two reasons: (1) The core values were never really put into practice, or (2) the values were only put in place as a "just in case." The truth is . . .

> Core values are not eye rolls.
> They are how the exceptional roll.

To survive these tumultuous business times, companies should look within and do a complete reassessment of their core values, which can be most helpful if you choose them carefully and use them properly.

Companies, from the top down, should *use* their values as modern decision-making filters when it comes to making difficult choices.

Think of them like bowling bumpers, those rails available on most lanes in bowling alleys. Most of us forget they're there, so we choose not to use them. But by using the bumpers, you have a mechanism in place to keep decisions out of the gutter. When it's time to make decisions, if you always have the bumpers active, you can continue to keep your decisions away from the danger zone and moving down the lane, toward your goal.

Your core values guide your decision making.

Having core values locked simplifies things, and it makes wrangling hard business choices just a little easier.

Susan David and Christina Congleton write in "Emotional Agility": "The mind's thought stream flows endlessly, and emotions change like the weather, but values can be called on at any time, in any situation."[1]

Businesses that know their core values know their truth.

Make every decision based on these truths. The things you value the most—these constants—should dictate all other decisions you make. And these core values should determine who you surround yourself with, what type of partners you work with, and the types of customers you look to attract.

You should even refer to your core values for hiring and firing.

Unfortunately, many companies miss the mark on what the next generation genuinely values. One major differentiator is that, with a surplus of choices at their fingertips, Millennials and Gen Zers won't join your company unless they are buying what you're selling. Eighty-five percent of Generation Z believe companies have an obligation to help solve social problems, while nearly 64 percent of Millennials and Gen Zers refuse to take a job if a potential employer doesn't have a rock-solid corporate social responsibility practice.[2] The way you can add value in their lives is by making it clear that you genuinely value your values.

And when you're joining a new company, do the diligence to make sure you can get on board with its values. Being aligned with the company's core values—whether you embraced them prior to joining the team or grew into them—brings unity and harmony.

Once these values are implemented, using them can also help steer you away from decisions that might be good for short-term success but detrimental for the long term. Chief marketing officer tenures have drastically dipped,[3] and often these positions of power are filled by new decision makers who step in and try to get a quick-hit win to establish credibility. But these short-sighted successes rarely have a positive impact on the company, specifically on the corporation's culture, in the long term.

How do we balance long- and short-term success? It starts by recognizing the importance of establishing a firm but fair stance both internally and externally based on your company's core values.

Ask Apple CEO Tim Cook. "If you want me to do things only for ROI reasons, you should get out of the stock," he said at a Q&A session at a 2014 stakeholder meeting.[4] It showed that Cook has values, values those values, and is empowered to represent and speak on behalf of the brand. Like an oak tree, Apple is rooted in rich, distinct core values that the company genuinely values, prioritizes, and practices regularly.

When your values are aligned with senior management, who trust you to make the right decisions on behalf of the business, you earn more freedom to make these decisions on your own. Building trust at the top empowers you to take charge. When you have that trust, you don't have to sacrifice the brand for short-term success.

Another way to build trust internally is to have the courage to move away from legacy values that may honor the founders of a historical company but that simply don't align with the changing times of our modern world.

When a company's leadership doesn't spend the time to dig deep and establish consequential and relevant core values that are respected and implemented from the top down, they are doing themselves, their teams, and their organization an enormous disservice.

PRIORITIZE YOUR VALUES

Since everything can't be a top priority, it's important to prioritize your values for the purpose of clarity and communication. This is why you must keep the most important values at the top of your values food chain—they must be the focal point.

This philosophy is best captured in that wonderful adage: "If everything is important, nothing is."

> The most important thing is the most important thing.

The most important thing only remains the most important thing when you prioritize it as such.

More so, if your teams can't rattle off your core values in a blink, you either chose too many or they aren't being enforced in the right manner. When you keep your core values focused to just a few, you are telling the world and your staff that you

1. Have prioritized which values matter most to you.

2. Know which critical values are your decision-making filters.

3. Strive to embody those select core values in everything you do as a company.

Core values will always bring you back to your mission. Having a mission attracts others who share that same mission. Companies that waver on this risk losing a reason for existing.

This raises the question about whether we as individuals have an awareness of what our personal core values are. You may have an idea of what matters most to you, but have you treated yourself like a business and done the hard work to examine and define what values you prioritize? This is especially important if you're trying to build your personal brand. Do you truly know yourself inside and out? Have you landed on personal core values you can rattle off if someone asks?

One of the most popular movies of my teenage years produced, in my opinion, one of the worst lines of counsel to an entire generation. In that famous *Jerry Maguire* surrender scene, Jerry gushes to single mother Dorothy, "You complete me."

I believe there is no "You complete me."
There is only "Me complete me."

There's absolutely no question that I'm better, and my life is better, because of my wife. That said, my wife and I do not complete each other. Rather, we complement each other. She complements me as much as I complement her. If we compromise too much, we both end up *compromised*.

Once we put in the work to know ourselves better, only then are we capable of sharing our distinct selves with one another.

Companies should follow suit. Businesses shouldn't try to be all things to all people. Rather, they should be all things to some people. Becoming OK with the fact that not everyone is your customer is a good thing. You'll be able to see that catering above and beyond to those who are your people is much easier.

Does the business know what it ultimately stands for? Is it unapologetic in knowing which customers it is and *isn't* for? Just like people, if a business is always compromising, trying to cast too wide of a consumer-nabbing net, it will be compromised. This is why it's critical to know *and* prioritize your values.

When you know who you are and what's important to you, you're also able to stay authentic to yourself and weather the storms of doubters, naysayers, and nonbelievers.

Mattress maker Tuft & Needle cofounder Daehee Park is not trying to be anyone but himself. "Pretty recently, it was recommended that we should get some media training," he says. "They want you to be polished, but maybe I'm not a polished person. I don't want to be a polished person. I don't think our employees would appreciate me trying to become a type of person that I'm not. It's so much easier to just talk about things I really believe in."[5]

When you stick to your values, uninformed people who disagree with you will likely come at you. The media may write about you. Employees will be dubious. Board members will question your decisions. To prepare for this friction, you need to clearly know who you are.

When you value your own values and prioritize those values, it means you have everything you need to weather these storms. Quite often your personal core values will differ from the values of the company you run. For example, my personal core values that help guide my decisions outside of work include:

- **Playfulness**: I take my work seriously but not myself.
- **Creativity**: It's my magic! Specifically, when solving business problems.
- **Courage**: And I do well with others who are courageous.
- **Excellence**: As lofty as it sounds, I aspire to do more with my time on this planet—and I am attracted to others in pursuit of excellence.

My special forces consultancy, Courageous, has a completely different set of four prioritized values. They are:

- **Relevance**: Our clients aspire to be thickly relevant; now and forever.
- **Sacrifice**: We help others make hard choices. Not everything can be the most important thing.
- **Speed**: We have the know-how and experience to urgently get the job done right.
- **Magic**: We're in the business of making people believe.

These core values of relevance, sacrifice, speed, and magic are always right there with us, not off in the distance, for when we need them. They authentically represent who we are as leaders and what we want for our company. These values help us make all our business decisions and are what matters most to us when it comes to our *culture*. All four help our staff know how to behave and what we expect of them on a daily basis. I even share these on Day 1 with prospects so they know how we intend to lead their business.

Note that it took me five years to figure out how important these were. Don't beat yourself up about not having these perfected right away. Keep tinkering until you get them right.

Of course, understanding who you are is only half the battle. Once you have that awareness, next is how you bring those values to life. Knowing your values and living them are not the same.

Amazon CEO Jeff Bezos, whose company leadership principles include customer obsession, invent and simplify, and hire and develop the best, says: "Your brand is formed primarily not by what your company says about itself, but what the company does."[6]

At Courageous, we live our values daily, monthly, and annually. Daily, we have our values leading off our client presentations and on every staff member's computer. Monthly, we reward members of our team who exemplify these values at staff meetings. That's 12 built-in times a year we are rewarding our all-stars with recognition and gift cards. Annually, we include our values as part of the hiring process, as well as on employee performance reviews.

Zappos has all ten of its core values listed on its employee key cards. Tyler Williams, a Zappos fungineer (yes, that's his title), says all the values are equally important, but one stands out from the rest. "I would say we identify externally the most with 'Deliver wow through service.'"[7] This isn't surprising with a company purpose statement of "To live and deliver wow." During the onboarding process, Zappos employees spend four weeks in its call center. It's how the company brings its top core value to life.

Everlane, a conscientious online fashion company, promotes radical transparency as a core value in all facets of its business—right down to the factories featured on its website. Most companies keep consumers in the dark about manufacturing partners; Everlane goes out of its way to do the opposite.

Harrah's Resort Southern California brings the core value of service to life with its Everyone Greets Everyone program, according to Darrell Pilant, the resort's senior vice president and general manager.

"When I arrived in October of 2011, I was surprised to find that when I walked by and said hello to a lot of employees, not many were returning the greeting,"[8] Pilant says.

In the beginning, Everyone Greets Everyone was an easy sell to the management team, but it wasn't as simple to implement with customer-facing teammates.

"As we all know, not everyone loves change," Pilant says. "The requirement was to greet everyone, teammates and customers, alike. It was a major change in culture for this resort. There was a lot of resistance at first, which is all but gone these days."

What at first was a suggestion by management became a structured mandate. Harrah's used its surveillance resources to monitor the program on a weekly basis. There was no margin for error. Anyone not greeting teammates or customers was held accountable, with disciplinary action for poor job performance. This was a team committed to making diamonds versus graphite.

Pilant says that after putting so much effort into enforcing the program, disciplinary action is now rare. "It's just a part of who we are," he says. "It took us about two years to get there, and it still needs constant attention, but anything that's a part of creating and maintaining a healthy culture does."

When it comes to service scores, Harrah's Resort Southern California ranks in the top four out of the 36 Caesars Entertainment properties. Management prioritized their core value and then took the necessary steps to make sure this value was present at all levels.

LIVE YOUR VALUES

Google's Jason Spero believes that "courage is being able to say a principle is a principle, regardless of your business reality. If you compete with people who are being more aggressive, your principles don't change."[9]

With the help of your values, you have the power to choose what your brand should or shouldn't take part in. The choices can be tough, but remember to look to your lighthouse.

Imagine you're the CEO of a well-known northeast airline. It's August 9, 2010. You learn that JetBlue Flight 1052 from Pittsburgh to New York City was pulling up to the gate when one of your flight attendants took it upon himself to address the 100 passengers over the public address system . . . drunk.

You then discover this flight attendant decided to complete his tirade over the intercom by woefully saluting your loyal travelers with the verbal version of the middle finger. And, as the plane finally arrived at the gate, he performed his *coup de grâce*; deploying the emergency exit door and evacuating himself, and the two beers in his hands, down the escape chute slide.[10]

Game. Set. Match. You are officially livid. A vein resembling the mighty Mississippi is fully exposed and runs down your head to your neck.

Many of you may be familiar with this story involving the "I'm not going to take it anymore" flight attendant Steven Slater.[11]

After allegedly getting hit in the head with a bag by a passenger prior to takeoff, Slater unsuccessfully requested an apology from the woman. From there, he snapped.

"I'm not proud of my actions in any way," says Slater, who, at the time of our interview in 2016, was living in a halfway house in Los Angeles. "What the world saw and thinks is a really funny moment is a terribly traumatic moment for me. It was a bipolar incident exacerbated by alcoholism and stress. It's a very shameful thing."

Slater was a seasoned air steward who had been flying the friendly skies for 20 years. He served TWA, Delta, and a few other airlines before landing at JetBlue in 2008. What most people don't know is that when this event occurred, his mother was undergoing chemotherapy on the West Coast and dying of cancer—it was an incredibly stressful time.

"I did not blow a slide and scream, 'F*** you,' because I was angry," he says. "I blew a slide and screamed, 'F*** you,' because I wasn't practicing self-care. I was so stressed out that I didn't have time to take care of myself. I wasn't going to my AA meetings. I wasn't taking the medication that I should have been. I didn't have time to care for me because I was too busy caring for a dying parent and trying to be a good model employee, which I was, up until that day."

Some could argue Slater was more than a mere model member of the workforce. According to Slater, he was chosen out of 1,200 JetBlue flight attendants, elected by his JetBlue peers, to represent the flight attendant group with management on what they call quality of life changes. He also says he was the chair of the Uniform Redesign Committee.

"I wasn't one of these disgruntled, angry people," he says. "I was literally the poster child. The marketing department was using me in advertisements. I was Mr. JetBlue."

The real Mr. JetBlue, then CEO David Barger, had his JetBlue flight delayed because of the infamous incident. No one can blame Barger and team for moving on from Slater.

There's no question that Slater's actions were wrong. He cost the airline a ton of mental anguish as well as some heavy financial tolls, including no less than a $10,000 hit just to replace the emergency slide. But what could their return on courage have been if JetBlue stood by its employee through the filter of its own core values? It's not until we review all five values that we wonder if they could have pursued a different path.

Slater effortlessly recalls JetBlue's values as if he were still a member of the force. "Passion, caring, integrity, safety, and fun. We were required to be able to rattle off the five core values at any given time."

Asked if JetBlue was living these values, Slater says, "From my vantage point, I was taking my mother to radiation every day in California and then driving 45 miles to LAX and sitting in the last row of coach on a red eye to travel back to New York to sleep two hours in the airport. Only to then work the red eye turn to San Juan, Puerto Rico, and come right back to sleep in the airport again, before jumping on another airplane to fly back to Los Angeles to take my mother back to chemotherapy."

Slater continues: "They knew that I was stressed. They knew that I was tired. They knew that I was suffering. To me, I don't feel a lot of compassion there. I don't see a lot of integrity after they denied my FMLA [Family and Medical Leave Act]."

According to Slater, he was first granted a base transfer to Los Angeles, which JetBlue subsequently rescinded before rejecting his FMLA request.

Slater continues, "If integrity matters, then you say, 'Well, you know what? This person has a dying parent. He's the primary caretaker. This parent is going to be dead within six months. Maybe we need to honor this base transfer.'"

Remember, you're the CEO of JetBlue. You have a massive, messy predicament on your hands. You're in the spotlight as you cope with an embarrassing and lengthy police investigation. Like it or not, this story is sticking with the public—some people are upset, and some are making fun of the situation. There is heavy media coverage. The world and your employees are watching your every move.

Right after the incident, Barger was quoted by *TheStreet* as saying, "Safety is the number one value at JetBlue," and deploying the chute was "an egregious act when you think about values."[12]

There is no doubt JetBlue has prioritized safety as its top core value. If you are truly living your core values, the first of which is safety, then making sure that all 100 passengers are safe comes first.

But once it declared its other four values as meaningful to the organization, no matter what circumstance it is faced with, it must also honor those values of passion, caring, integrity, and fun.

What if JetBlue had approached this situation with Steven Slater differently? What if the company had used it as an opportunity to flip the situation from hapless to hopeful? To show the world how caring the company truly is. How integrity matters so much that it's just as important to safely rehabilitate a wounded, (once) loyal employee.

Here's how I would have handled the situation.

I would have called a press conference, with Slater by my side. I would have notified the media that all 100 passengers would be receiving round-trip complimentary tickets to anywhere in the continental United States (fun!).

I would have suggested that my employee of 20 years, who did make some very bad choices, was clearly having a bad day. Slater apologizes on air and reveals he's checked himself into rehab, which I would have paid for. I would have then explained to the media that we don't condone Slater's behavior and that it won't be tolerated again. Then, with conviction, I would have followed that up with, "We passionately stand by our employee. We're going to make sure that he gets counseling, we're going to take care of him, and he's not going to come back until he's rehabilitated; but when he's better and ready, he's going to return to his JetBlue family."

It sure is easy to Monday morning quarterback this difficult situation well after the fact. But this is just one way JetBlue could have gone about diffusing a difficult moment in its history. Leadership could have taken a remarkably tough moment and courageously showcased how they are living their five declared core values. Nothing to roll your eyes about here.

Though it's tough not to waver when much of the world is watching, this scenario would send a clear, strong message to your employees, your empathetic customers, and your stakeholders that your core values are important, and you live by them. And if you ask me, that demonstration of humanity would have earned more than a round of applause: It would have been a resounding *Return on Courage.*

THE VALUES ARROW

It's not enough to know your values. You have to live them. Don't let your core values become nothing more than antiquated sideline values. Don't allow your values to simply become meaningless fodder— merely wallpaper art on a lobby wall.

Your values can be your company's best friend, something your team can rely on during every decision and offering regarding your business.

This is what I call the *Values Arrow* at work.

The Values Arrow starts with your core values, then it goes straight through your beliefs, your staff, your offerings, and your message. This message carries through to your customers and, if the message is meaningful enough, to your customers' networks.

THE VALUES ARROW:

- Your Values
- Your Staff
- Your Offerings

- Your Message

- Your Customers

- Your Customers' Networks

The *P* in P.R.I.C.E. (Prioritizing through values) is the first and most critical step for any company looking to build a strong, healthy Central Courage System.

Knowing and prioritizing your values is knowledge.

Valuing your values is a version of faith.

Living your values is a form of action.

Now that we have total appreciation of what we value, it's time to find and align with others who do, too. When we talk about the Values Arrow running through our staff, we land squarely on the second part of P.R.I.C.E.:

Rallying Believers.

PRIORITIZE THROUGH VALUES WORKSHEET

IT IS TIME to take these concepts and put them into practice. Utilize the space below or grab a notebook and let's dig deeper into your values—both personal and business. (After all, one should be a reflection of the other!)

1. **Treat yourself like a brand. Write down three to five personal core values.**

   Once you know what matters most to you, only then are you truly equipped to make fast, calculated decisions in your life. These decisions include who to surround yourself with as much as what to spend your time on. If you have business partners, have them do the same exercise on their own. Note: Don't hesitate to write down more than five potential values and then pare your list down to your core three to five. Drawing a blank already? It's OK; there is a Values Master List in the Appendix C of this book on page 211.

   a.

   b.

c.

d.

e.

2. **Write down your company core values. Does each one pass the modern sniff test? Do you have a "just in case" value on your list? Circle the one or two values that might need replacing. Look to exchange it for something that helps you drive a desired behavior of the team.**

    A "just in case" value is something that you feel you need (like a CYA value or a legacy value), but it doesn't truly instigate the type of action you desire from your staff. These types of values hold you back, dilute your focus, and take unnecessary time away from those core beliefs that truly drive behavior.

    a.

    b.

    c.

    d.

    e.

3. **Prioritize your core values list, leading with the most important.**

    What matters most to you? Second most? And so on. When you think about a critical decision that needs to be made on behalf of the organization, vet it through these core values. Get total clarity on what you believe to be the most important thing to your company. Since this is a personal belief, this will be different for everyone! Remember to share with your immediate team to discuss what is (and isn't) working for them.

a.

b.

c.

d.

e.

4. **Now that you know what matters most, how will you transfer your core values into guiding principles?**

Invite your partners/senior management to participate in this exercise. Share your prioritized core values and don't be afraid to get personal. Perhaps write each team member's values on a white board. From there, work hard to crystallize these into three to five aligned guiding principles. These guiding principles should be used to drive the desired behavior of your internal team.

a.

b.

c.

d.

e.

5. **How can you use your core values in decision making? Write down three everyday work scenarios in which you should turn to your values/principles to make decisions.**

One of the benefits of completing this exercise is to use your core values as decision-making filters. They might be invoked to set the tone during orientation with a new staff member or during a prospecting call with a potential new client. How do you want your values to guide these moments?

   a.

   b.

   c.

6. **How will you bring your company core values to life throughout your organization? Write down how you will implement these values with coworkers monthly and/or annually.**

How can you make it possible for all of your employees to see what values matter most to the organization? Are you rewarding people for their behavior at staff meetings or monthly corporate events? Have you included the values/principles in performance reviews? Are the values on a keycard, on a visible wall, or hanging up at your employees' desks? This exercise will help you activate the values company-wide.

   a.

   b.

   c.

RALLY BELIEVERS

"They must believe in the cause for which they are
fighting. They must believe in the plan they are asked
to execute, and most important, they must believe in
and trust the leader they are asked to follow."[1]
—Jocko Willink and Leif Babin, Navy SEALs

LET'S SAY THAT your boss is disconnected from the day-to-day happenings at your company. They continue to make big decisions without consulting the team. You become confused and wonder why this is happening.

Now, your attention isn't on doing the right thing for the business but on how to stop the wrong thing your boss has put in play.

At night, you have trouble sleeping, and you realize that you have two choices: You can go with the flow and not say anything, or you can try to address this problem with your boss. This will be a daunting task and difficult to explain, and it could be a huge risk to your livelihood.

Your mind drifts again. You begin to ponder if this is the right place for you. You wonder why you care so much. The easy thing to do is just care *less*. Your faith has wavered.

This inner conversation happens to many of us in our working lives, and when it does, we are officially no longer a believer.

Building a successful business culture is more art than science. This chapter focuses on creating, retaining, and sustaining internal believers.

Why is this so important? Because believers aren't just wanted, they are needed to rally *Believers*. To do this, you must surround yourself with others who rightfully buy in to the values, purpose, offerings, and people of the organization.

Making Believers all starts at the top with what I call your *Believership*.

THE BELIEVERSHIP

To be followed you need to lead well. The clear mission of leadership is to become the company's Believership.

The sole purpose of your Believership is to create Believers out of your board, employees, prospects, and customers.

Internal discord begins the minute your staff starts questioning and calling out your faulty decisions.

Management guru Ken Blanchard is spot on when he writes, "It takes a whole team of people to create a great company but just one lousy leader to take the whole business down the pan."[2]

> Poor leaders often misconstrue leadership
> as cheerleadership.

Leaders who cheerlead to their staff are not effective leaders. Their pick-me-up intentions, especially when times are tough, often come from the right place. Yet these types of leaders often avoid sharing the hardest, truest information with their team for fear of breaking morale. These antics may win over a subset of the staff, but usually your seasoned employees can smell when they are not receiving your truth.

This is one of the main reasons I prefer Believership over leadership.

The Believership sets the tone for the entire company. They may deliver bad news from time to time, but they never give the team something to question; they always take the high road and prioritize what the company needs, even when it's hard. Having a leader who makes it easy for employees to believe remains the difference. This is about setting the vision, delivering the truth no matter how hard the circumstance, and surrounding yourself with a team that is authentically aligned.

Successfully leading is not simply about one person, though. Your Believership should be a mixture of different types of unique personalities who all abide by the company's core values.

As cofounders of direct-to-consumer mattress company Tuft & Needle, Daehee Park and JT Marino form the Believership of their company. When it comes to their Believership, Marino is more likely to dream up innovative ideas while Park grounds those concepts in reality.

"I oversee and work with finance, legal, and marketing," Park says. "JT takes the same approach with product development, software, and retail."[3]

The more they work together, the more they respect the different skills each brings to the table.

"The reason we believe it works is because we have opposite personalities and yet share the same values and goals for the company— what we want to work on and how we want to represent ourselves," Park says.

Park and Marino met in college and have the distinct advantage of knowing each other very well. Though it's not always realistic, we all prefer to work with people we like and who we've succeeded with in the past. When any of us move to a new company, especially when we're in a position of power, we try to cajole these intelligent allies to join us. This is because we trust them. Trust is the most essential ingredient of any successful team and the key component for identifying ideal candidates to join a Believership team.

When you're forming your Believership, you should remember that the size of your Believership matters. The smaller the group, the easier it should be to keep that team on track and aligned. If your Believership is too big, the motives of the group will begin to change. As organizational health guru Patrick Lencioni suggests, "When groups are more than eight or nine people, people get concerned that they won't get the floor again."[4]

Fender chief marketing officer Evan Jones says this of his Believership team: "You don't last in the band if you're not willing to listen to what other people are playing. I'd say when it comes to the brand's direction, there are five of us—our CEO, CFO, head of core products, head of digital products, and me. Everyone is aligned at that level."[5]

Jones calls the Fender Believership extremely vulnerable and transparent. "What's interesting about this place is, because we have a lot of ex-musicians and artists, trust is critical," he says. "You need that when you're trying to do daunting tasks, especially attempting to build a new road map."

Jones admits that he has brought in people he has previously worked with and already had confidence in because of those past work experiences. These people are now critical to bringing the future Fender to life.

At San Francisco soap company Method, the team dynamic was diversified but tight from the get-go. Cofounder Eric Ryan calls it "getting the balance right," by bringing together business and design thinking—an artist and an operator model. "Cofounder Adam Lowry and I acted as artists in setting the vision," Ryan says. "Drew Fraser [who is now the president and CEO of Method] was better at executing."[6]

Ryan and his Believership also chose to have an external advisory board to bounce ideas off of. This proficient resource of three didn't derail the inner workings of the internal organization, and when it came time to share decisions to Method's internal Believers, Ryan was the one who delivered the news.

Ryan was Method's Chief Belief Officer.

CHIEF BELIEF OFFICER

Many Believerships have Chief Belief Officers. They are living, breathing *raisons d'être*. They're company soul-setters like Michael Dubin from Dollar Shave Club, Richard Branson from Virgin, and Blake Mycoskie from TOMS shoes. They are Sheryl Sandberg from Facebook, Tim Cook from Apple, and Jeff Bezos from Amazon.

The face of the company should be a face that consumers know.

"The difference between Gillette and Dollar Shave Club is that Dollar Shave Club has Michael [Dubin] who is the face of the brand and still talking to you like the founder of the company who believed in what he is saying," Tuft & Needle's Park says. "Gillette would never be able to do that. What kind of spokesperson are they going to put in front of you that's real and authentic?"[7]

As the face of your company, the Chief Belief Officer (CBO) takes on the responsibility of being front and center with staff, customers, and the public. The Believership believes in the CBO calling the shots, and on the flip side, the CBO must fully believe in the members of the Believership. Hiding behind press releases or the brand is not the way to breed courageous internal behavior.

We buy in because the CBO's vision is strong; this person is authentic and worth following. When you have the right CBO and the right Believership, there's a higher likelihood you'll make Believers.

Companies either *make* Believers or *fake* Believers.

There are many ways to make Believers out of your team.

Steve Jobs always preferred to construct small teams of A-plus players. Jack Williams brought many trusted players with him from his successful days at American Airlines to Royal Caribbean. When Domino's president Russell Weiner moved from Pepsi, he took great pride in keeping the team he inherited in his first year as chief marketing officer. Pete Carroll reportedly rattled through 200 players to find the right mix of players in his first season as the coach of the Seattle Seahawks.[8]

No matter how you go about building your cohesive team, the question you must ask yourself in the end is *Did you make them Believers?*

The good CBOs know how important it is to get their story right to the external world. The great CBOs know how important it is to get it right first for their employees. Courage Brands do not have a public and private persona. They are one and the same. Many Courage Brands smartly treat their employees just as well if not better than their customers.

CREATING BELIEVERS

Employees today need to buy in to what your company is selling. If they don't buy in, they will leave. If they leave your company, out walks your company's institutional knowledge. As we learned earlier, when your talent moves on, you've just disrupted the dynamic of your team.

You must also consider your future internal Believers—those misunderstood Millennials. Many perceive them to be entitled. This is, frankly, irrelevant. Deloitte reports that by 2025, Millennials will make up 75 percent of our global workforce.[9]

Kiely & Co. founder Katz Kiely has been studying our future talent. "They display different behaviors and have different expectations and needs," she writes of Millennials. "Company loyalty cannot be expected, it has to be earned, and financial compensation is only part of the package."[10]

Many are missing the mark as to what this purpose-centric generation really values. Millennials are looking to have their cake and eat it, too—but the cake must also be gluten-free. They want to be a part of something they believe in.

"The focus is moving away from competitive processes toward collaborative goals," Kiely adds. "Leaders know they need to move from the 'I' to the 'we,' toward continuous feedback and improvement and agility to be an employer of choice."

Jeff Ragovin, a cofounder of Buddy Media, says, "It's a red flag when an employee says, 'Yeah, OK, it's a job where I'm making some money, but I'm not going to put my values on the line for something that I wholeheartedly don't believe in.'"[11]

This is in line with Millennial thinking. They aspire to work for values-based companies that set out to make better products and a better world. They want it all, including being part of tight-knit teams working on meaningful projects for impassioned leaders.

Millennials don't want to work at a place they don't believe in. Speaking from experience, having an optimal culture translates into having optimal Millennials.

This is critical to keep in mind as you create a *Believership* team who can empower your next workforce. The good news is that you don't have to wait a decade to start making Believers out of your staff today.

There are four ways to Make Believers:

- Respecting Makes Believers.
- Repeating Makes Believers.
- Caring Makes Believers.
- Seeing Is Believing.

Respecting Makes Believers

One way to make an internal Believer is by moving away from the old-school management style of command and control. When you trust your team to manage its time wisely without having to rule with an iron fist, that's when the magic happens.

Google is a textbook case. One of the global leaders in hiring top talent, Google respects staff and gives employees breathing room. Many are aware of Google's 20 percent rule. This is the allocation of 20 percent of employees' work time to follow their own personal projects that can breed future Google innovations. Some estimate up to half of all new Google products come from employees flexing the 20 percent rule. Google Sky, a feature of Google Earth, is one example.

This is respecting your team.

Often, we need to let go to grow. If you have the right team in place, your best bet is to provide detailed instruction and get out of the way so the team can deliver. This becomes an issue if we give poor instruction about expectations, so make sure expectations are set from the get-go.

Verne Harnish, author of the leadership book *Scaling Up*, put it well when he wrote, "Many leaders confuse delegation with abdication.

Abdication is blindly handing over a task to someone with no formal feedback mechanism. Letting go and trusting others to do things well is one of the more challenging aspects of being a leader of a growing organization."[12]

When you properly give your teams the green light to freely do their jobs, you create employees who will be advocates. You give these new Believers permission to make other Believers.

Respecting your team also means giving them daunting tasks—not to be confused with *tedious* tasks. Believers believe because they are constantly challenged. They're pushed and inspired by the Believership with difficult, meaningful projects. These are the assignments where courage plays a major role. Believers take pride in being responsible for these types of projects by the Believership. They feel lucky to work at the companies they proudly represent.

American entrepreneur and philanthropist Peter Thiel notes how Elon Musk set "the specialness" tone for his elite staff.

"Elon describes his staff this way," Thiel says. "If you're at Tesla, you're choosing to be at the equivalent of Special Forces."[13]

How do you know if you have staff who are Believership worthy? When they are willing to bet on themselves. Embrace the specialness of these willing people. When you run into unique, proactive types, bring them onto your team and partner them with like-minded, committed people.

Repeating Makes Believers

This isn't the same as an anonymous salesperson flooding your inbox with a constant barrage of the same message over and over again. Thankfully, the death of that salesman has finally arrived.

This is a different type of repeating.

Repeating Makes Believers is all about clarity and alignment.

Not only does your staff want to hear from your CBO, they also want to hear the same precise message being delivered from each member of the Believership. Like a beating drum, all senior parties need to repeat the same themes over and over until employees internalize their rhythm.

When we repeat ourselves, we provide the necessary cadence of consistent commentary that keeps our teams sane.

Research maverick and author Jim Collins suggests the signature of a pedestrian company is chronic inconsistency.[14] This means that when companies incessantly change their internal message they exhaust and overwhelm their staff.

Amazon brand category leader Andrew Turner attributes a huge part of his successful career to seven years of ups and downs at Eddie Bauer. "There was a period of time there that we were white hot and when we leaned into those things that were aligned with our core values, we were executing flawlessly and purposely, and people believed it," he recalls. "We were high-caliber, we were clicking, people were in the zone, and then the players changed. You lose some people and management shifts, and then it kind of goes away."[15]

Skepticism fades with repetition of the same message because it creates something constant your team can reliably count on. As a staff sponges up the same message from multiple people and it becomes familiar over time, they begin to accept it. Once accepted, all that time and energy can be channeled squarely on the task at hand.

Caring Makes Believers

It's as simple as this: Believing in the people around you makes it easier for them to believe in you.

Sometimes, this means courageously opening up and embracing your humanity. Many of my friends from corporate America are concerned about watching their backs when, of course, they'd rather be in a got-your-back culture. As Teddy Roosevelt once said: "People do not care how much you know, until they know how much you care."[16]

Genuine relationships make the business world go round. You have to know your people inside and out. Take the time to learn about your superiors, your peers, and your coworkers. Get to know where they are from and where they went to school. Ask them about their families, hobbies, and what sports teams they like. Showing interest in your people and getting to know what matters most to them can only bring you closer together and make things more personal. Otherwise, you're living in a mere transactional relationship, versus a transformational one.

Crafting a two-way relationship is just another way to forge trust. As we've already learned; without trust, it's hard to make a true Believer.

Jeff Ragovin kept that trust with the team at Buddy Media. "We believed in the people that we hired—we made sure they all knew how much we believed in them."

Ragovin and team leave nothing to the imagination. "If no one ever mentions that you're doing amazing things, it's not really a good feeling because you're not getting any type of positive reinforcement. You're actually getting—believe it or not—negative reinforcement by [supervisors] not saying anything."[17]

Go ahead and share with your staff when they are doing great. Share with your full team, town hall style, when they are performing. When you care enough to share, especially in a public forum, you deliver a lasting emotional reward that creates true loyalty.

Seeing Is Believing

You've heard the phrase, "If you see something, say something." In business, it's the opposite: If you say something, your staff must see something. Make sure you deliver on your word—that everyone sees the change you said you'd make. The courage to do what needs to be done isn't easy.

Go back to the JetBlue "live your values" story. If you say you stand for caring, act out that core value in everything you do, even when it's hard.

Talk is cheap. As we all should know by now, actions speak louder than words. If you say something, you must follow through.

I remember a time when my company moved on from a less-than-courageous client because they asked us to do something that violated our core values. Most of our staff had already known that this client wasn't particularly aligned with our values. When our Believership team finally announced the news to our staff, it instantly brought us all together.

Seeing Is Believing also pays homage to making progress on something truly original. Many have questioned Elon Musk's shoot-for-the-moon goals for SpaceX. When his team sees ambitious progress with their own eyes, though, they believe. They believe they are on a cultural rocket ship in a company that's building rocket ships.

When you see something truly courageous, even in small doses, you begin to believe.

Joe Bellezzo, chair of emergency medicine at Sharp Memorial Hospital in San Diego, believes this concept rings true with breakthrough medical procedures as well. His elite group of emergency room doctors may be the only team in the Western Hemisphere successfully bringing to life heart–lung bypasses in the ER.

"The whole team now believes in this because we've accomplished something pretty remarkable, even if it's just once or twice," Bellezzo says. "If you really believe something can work, its chances of survival are much better than if you don't believe in it."[18]

FAKE BELIEVERS

Believers are always watching what the Believership does. If they like what they see, they remain Believers. If they don't, if they have lost faith in their boss or senior management's ability to make sound decisions, they will often start saying bad things about the company outside of work.

These Fake Believers roaming around your organization are toxic and spread negativity. They are putting the company mission in jeopardy and creating holes in the corporate dam that will eventually cause larger problems on your dime and on your time. This is where productivity diminishes and side conversations flourish.

Once you have Fake Believers, motivation drops and efficiency plummets.

It's important to note that Fake Believers are not bad people. They are just in the wrong place. Fake Believers should go work for people they can believe in.

If you find yourself doubting what you see around you and you have trouble believing in the company you spend so much time at, perhaps it's time to move on. If you can't share that common positive sentiment with your current company, maybe it's time to start looking for something more personally meaningful.

Or maybe you should make the courageous choice to address this with a superior. The truth may set you free just like courage sets you free.

Naturally, it's hard to share these truths with superiors or upper management. It's hard to go against what's accepted as truth. But not saying anything when you disagree is how Fake Believers are made.

It's hard to let go of someone who *doesn't* fit anymore. When this is the case, ask yourself what is in the absolute best interest of the business.

When you put what's right for the business first, no matter how hard it is, the right decision will rise to the surface. When you don't make the right decision, you may find yourself with a handful of Believers who watched you keep someone who is slowing the rest of the team down, which is just another way to make Fake Believers.

So how can you tell the difference between a Believer and a Fake Believer? Just look at how they choose to show up, how available they make themselves, and how they play the game.

What does this have to do with making courageous decisions?

When the Believership is totally aligned, has mutual respect for staff, shows employees they regularly care, and follows through on their word, they have rallied a united and focused team of loyal Believers. It puts the company on a path to creating an encouraged workforce versus a discouraged workforce. And it's the difference between having a "got your back" culture versus a "watch your back" culture.

Remember, the Believership's sole goal is to make Believers in everything they do. A staff of committed Believers will work harder for your Believership team and will wholeheartedly carry out the cause of your company with conviction.

You will need those united Believers to combat the mortifying truths of the Business Apocalypse. Together, you can confront those complicated difficulties that pummel unprepared companies into eventual irrelevance.

RALLY BELIEVERS WORKSHEET

ORGANIZATIONS CREATE BELIEVERS or Fake Believers. Now that you know what your company stands for, it is time to surround yourself with Believers! These are other like-minded people who are committed to living out the values and purpose of the company.

At the top, the Believership is a collection of individuals responsible for driving your business and culture forward. These are the people in your organization who model the behavior, the decisions, and the values you want the rest of your employees to emulate.

1. **Who is in your company's Believership? List three to nine people.**

A healthy, functioning Believership is a collection of internal leaders who are aligned on the agreed-upon values but can be composed of multiple titles, levels, and points of view. Your Believership team should represent the breadth of your company. (Note: Beyond nine people, the intention of the group can get muddled.)

    a.

    b.

c.

d.

e.

f.

g.

h.

i.

2. **Of your Believership list, who is the Chief Belief Officer?**

The Chief Belief Officer (CBO) is not only the leader of the Believership, but also the recognizable face of the company. This person must be authentic and worth following. Remember, this book is about having the courage to change. Don't have a CBO (or have the wrong one)? Who internally creates conviction? Who is the right person that employees would be willing to follow? Finally, why did you choose that person? What is it about them that makes a Believer out of you and others?

a.

3. **How can your Believership make Believers in all directions? List three to five ways.**

Remember, there are four ways to make a Believer: respecting, repeating, caring, and seeing is believing. Audit the things your current Believership is doing well. (For example, communicating the same message regularly and as a unit. Empowering decisions. Leading by example.

Rewarding staff monthly through recognition or rewards.) If you were part of the Believership, list three to five ways you would make Believers inside your organization. Setting aside internal hurdles, what would you implement to win the team over?

a.

b.

c.

4. **Who else in your company would make good candidates for your Believership? List three to five people and why.**

Your business is not just about today, but tomorrow as well. Who are you going to foster into future Believership positions? Remember, this has nothing to do with current title or age. We're just looking for future all-stars who are (1) tenacious, (2) about the team, and (3) have the talent.

a.

b.

c.

d.

e.

5. **External to your company, who else have you worked with that would be good additions to your Believership? List two people and why.**

List two people with whom you once worked that you know and like who would be ideal Believership candidates now or in the future. This is important to share as it may reveal what traits or characteristics are missing from your existing Believership.

   a.

   b.

IDENTIFY FEARS

"I'm not a daredevil. I don't do skydiving.
I'm afraid of heights."
—Reed Timmer, Tornado Chaser

REED TIMMER IS an extreme meteorologist with a mad passion for hunting storms. For nearly two decades, Timmer, who studied meteorology at the University of Oklahoma, has pursued tornadoes. His Discovery Channel show was called *Storm Chasers.*

"I've loved weather ever since I was probably five years old," Timmer says. "I used to get fired up when severe storms or warnings would get issued in Michigan, where I grew up. I'd run all around the house trying to steal the family video camera and shoot videos of big hailstorms coming in."[1]

The seasoned storm chaser believes that every storm is uniquely different. The more time he spent studying tornadoes, the more he learned how each storm behaved. Now, when it comes to running right at these furious funnels, Timmer is not afraid to admit he's not afraid.

"I understand storms. People that are afraid of storms have probably never learned about them. Honestly, when I'm storm chasing, I never feel in danger. Fear is relative."

Timmer admits he has had a few too-close-for-comfort calls.

"I've taken some risks and gotten a little closer than I should have," he says. "I think a lot of it is based on the knowledge and the experience that you've gained storm chasing; you can read the storm, understand it, and know when to seize the opportunity."

When Timmer passionately discusses these opportunities, his deep knowledge shows.

"To get close to a tornado, I'll approach from the up-shear direction. They like to wobble left and right of that axis," he says. "They can expand rapidly down-shear. I'll punch from west to east through that rain and then gain a visual of the wall cloud or tornado to my south. That was something I learned through years and years of storm chasing, getting myself in bad spots, learning from it, and correcting my approach. It took a lot of years to perfect the science of getting close to tornadoes."

After two decades, the luster of calling it courageous has faded, but Timmer's enthusiasm remains the same. Instead of running from his fear, Timmer, armed with knowledge, goes right at it. He has faith that things will turn out all right. When he's in a storm, he has to pivot as new information presents itself in real time. He adds that to his knowledge bank and adjusts his actions appropriately.

What can we learn from Timmer when we translate this type of thinking into the workplace? When the twister is lurking near our business, do we run the other way? Or should we inch closer and learn everything we can to chase down our fears?

"Fear is the thief of dreams," author and journalist Brian Krans suggests.[2]

Fear chokes us up and holds us back. Fear shackles us to the status quo where we feel secure and convinces us to avoid controversial action and hard conversations. Fear fuels paralysis and empowers unwanted procrastination.

Susan David and Christina Congleton wrote in *Harvard Business Review,* "The prevailing wisdom says that negative thoughts and feelings have no place at the office. But that goes against basic biology. All healthy human beings have an inner stream of thoughts and feelings that include criticism, doubt and fear."[3]

Fear is as normal as the air we breathe. Yet when we are afraid, it feels as if we can't breathe.

So why are we so fearful of an emotion that every human on the planet experiences?

Some believe the word *fear* stands for "false evidence appearing real." Fear fuels our speculation, making it easy for us to freak ourselves out. That trepidation paints fictitious ugly portraits played out in our minds as failures or firings.

But we have to deal with it.

As the famous proverb reminds us, "Fear and courage are brothers." We can't achieve courage without channeling it first through our fear.

Once we Prioritize through Values, and Rally Believers, which are the organizational health steps of building a strong and functioning Central Courage System, we can then begin to tackle the next step of P.R.I.C.E.: Identifying Fears.

ADDRESS FEARS, DON'T SUPPRESS FEARS

Successful businesses, led by their Believership, overtly unearth, then call out, their largest fears—addressing them versus suppressing them—with their believing staff. This Believership will do everything in its power to shine a light on and address these business fears head-on.

When we identify fears, we begin the process of conquering our most complicated business problems. We can drum up courageous solutions that shrink these progress-halting, nightmare hurdles.

> To address your fear is to know your fear.
> Don't steer clear of it; address it head-on.

Loretta Hidalgo is a founding astronaut at Virgin Galactic and has always been passionate about going to space. "It goes back as far as I can remember, but I can date it to six years old," she says. "People who are in our industry chose to be here. They were 'called' to be here. It is something that binds us together; it's a unifier."[4]

Hidalgo reminds us that it's not easy to be an astronaut. "In our industry, people can die," she says. "There's a lot more at stake than when you are coding an app. When we screw up computer code, people die. It's one thing that's intense about our industry: It's really real. You have to face that."

Other feelings she's had to face? Fear.

"Fear is just a piece of information," she says. "It's evolutionary—created to protect you. Just think, 'Thank you, evolution, for trying to keep me safe,' but I need to be here right now. It's living by choice rather than survival. Fear is your friend. It's not trying to hurt you."

If fear is not trying to hurt you, it's here to assist you. Fear can be helpful. Not irrational fear, but fear that aids you during those high-pressure, stressful moments. On the business front, fear is that nagging dull pain in your gut that tells you, "Hey, this matters, and you better figure it out or you're finished." Fear can be an incredibly powerful tool when it comes to recognizing what's important.

So how do you go about harnessing fear in a useful way?

"You have to learn to assess it," Hidalgo says. "Ask yourself, 'Am I really in danger?' You can use it to be more aware. Fear makes you hyper present, and that's quite useful."

Imagine presenting to the "Greatest Showman on Earth"—the CEO of Ringling Bros. I have never been more terrified in my creative life than presenting to Kenneth Feld and his team. For 90 minutes, it was as if I was on a metaphorical unicycle juggling fire as I presented potential names and concepts for their magical Ringling Bros. and Barnum & Bailey Circus. Though I could feel my fear, I knew I was as *prepared* as I could be for this moment. And, in the end, we agreed on a show title and concept. Successfully powering through that frightening experience made every other presentation moving forward in my career just a little bit easier because I had become a bit more familiar with something once unfamiliar.

Perhaps business is more about finding fear than fighting fear. Treat fear like an object buried in the ground. Dig it out and bring it to the surface. If you don't think you have a fear, dig deeper and identify a potential fear that could affect you in the future.

Every company should have a potential future fear because fear leads to growth.

Exposing then addressing that fear forces examination and an action plan. It can kick-start innovation. It can help you fight your way back to relevancy. That fear can be flipped into your friend.

There are four types of business fears companies may face:

1. Industry Fears

2. Product Fears

3. Service Fears

4. Perception Fears

Since businesses are nothing more than shells full of people, we must also discuss the realities of the decision-altering, mind-freezing personal fears.

Courage Brands discuss the consequences of letting any of these fears run unchecked. It makes defeating a fear feel inevitable by aggressively shrinking it and chipping away at its weakness.

INDUSTRY FEARS

For 80 years, people grossly underestimated the demand of public transportation. Then came ridesharing. Calling on Siri now usurps dialing 411. The majority of us scour search engines like Google rather than flipping through the Yellow Pages. And the rise of Netflix brought the curtain down on Blockbuster.

Jonathan Salem Baskin, who was the senior vice president in Corporate Relations at Blockbuster, wrote a *Forbes* article suggesting the thing that killed Blockbuster was not Netflix or the Internet but Blockbuster itself. "Blockbuster could have written a business school case on its reinvention, and who knows what role it could have crafted for itself this decade, or beyond?" Baskin wrote. "It could have owned the position of movie experts and migrated that brand to any new distribution platform."[5]

We already know how this movie ends.

Netflix, with a track record for reinvention, became the industry fear for Blockbuster. Ironically, in 2000, Netflix was offered for acquisition to Blockbuster for $50 million, but Blockbuster declined. Fourteen years later, Netflix had 50 million global subscribers and held just under a third of the entire streaming market. In the fourth quarter of 2015, Netflix was considered the leading US-based television "network" according to the chief research officer at Turner Broadcasting System.[6]

Are you still relevant in your industry today? Did someone figure out a better way to position, market, and outsell a product or service that revolutionized your industry? If so, what's next for you?

Ask yourself, do you have an industry fear,
or can you be an industry fear?

Lou Gerstner once wrote about IBM's industry fears: "In prior incarnations, my management team and I could identify four or five companies or organizations that had been our competitors for the past twenty years and would probably continue to be our competitors for the next twenty. In the information technology industry, literally thousands of new competitors sprang up every year—some in garages, some in universities, some in the hearts and minds of brilliant entrepreneurs."[7]

These undeclared and unforeseen companies I call *Industry Blind Spots.*

These lurking, ambitious competitors that have yet to make themselves known are the ones we all need to watch out for. These ambitious companies are nowhere on our radar, but they're probably relentlessly planning an attack out of an MBA dorm room or Silicon Valley garage.

Industry blind spots are tomorrow's
potential hotshots.

Warby Parker cofounders Neil Blumenthal and David Gilboa addressed a deck full of entrepreneurs at the Summit at Sea in November 2015. Asked what keeps them up at night, Gilboa responded: "There are probably four guys in a dorm room trying to figure out how to take us down."[8]

I took this as a confident admission of their being able to handle anything in the category that had already made itself known. What could knock them off was an industry blind spot that had yet to reveal itself.

When you are a known entity in an established category, focused purely on protecting what you already have, you land yourself in a position where you could suffer from an industry blind spot. You may think you are untouchable, but you aren't. None of us are.

Many hotels are a good example. Hotel brands spent a great deal of their time monitoring what other hotel brands are doing. Then along came Airbnb. "Fear and conservative thinking is holding back the growth of a lot of traditional organizations," says Jonathan Mildenhall, chief marketing officer at Airbnb.[9]

It's hard to predict what may happen if you don't build in processes to plan for industry blind spots. When these future competitors finally make themselves known, they often force businesses into reactionary mode, and then it may be too late.

So how on earth can you look for something that doesn't exist?

Wharton business professor Adam Grant wrote in his best-selling book *Originals*, "At the pharmaceutical giant Merck, CEO Kenneth Frazier decided to motivate his executives to take a more active role in leading innovation and change. He asked them to do something radical: generate ideas that would put Merck out of business. For the next two hours, the executives worked in groups, pretending to be one of Merck's top competitors. Energy soared as they developed ideas for drugs that would crush theirs and key markets they had missed. Then, their challenge was to reverse their roles and figure out how to defend against these threats."[10]

Though you'll never be able to have all the knowledge and see all the potential pitfalls, running this exercise will allow you to make the most of the intelligence you do have.

Consider putting your Believership team through this "take the company down" thinking at an off-site meeting. When you don't plan for the competitors you don't know, it may be too late to properly address them when they finally emerge.

PRODUCT FEARS

From 1997 to 2005, Jack Williams was president and chief operating officer at Royal Caribbean Cruises. When he took the job at 47 years of age, he was one of the youngest heads of a Fortune 500 company.[11]

When Williams was hired, brought on by CEO Richard Fain, the company had just embarked on a huge risk with its product by creating cruise ships that were double the size of the previous fleet. At the time, 80,000-gross-registered-ton (GRT) sovereign-class ships were the norm. But Royal Caribbean was planning to build a 170,000-GRT experience.

"It was a big gamble," Williams says. "We bet the balance sheet. If the Voyager Class ship didn't work, it was over for that company. It would have been over."

There was no plan B. There was no alternate route. There were, Williams says, a lot of sleepless nights.

Two to three weeks before launching the giant new ship, Williams and Fain were worried about how their customers were going to accept this experience. They were scared that this ship was going to be perceived as a giant shopping mall at sea.

Courage always starts with knowledge. And there was a lot of knowledge going into the plan.

Williams recalls, "You have to remember that at the time there were only about eight to ten million people cruising. We weren't trying to compete with Princess, Carnival, Holland, or Celebrity. We weren't going to make a company successful because we got more people to migrate from a Carnival experience to a Royal Caribbean experience. Our success was going to get land-based vacationers to sea—getting people out of Disneyland, getting people out of Las Vegas, and getting them out to sea."

When Royal Caribbean built the Voyager Class ship, research

showed there were 30 to 40 million people sitting on the fence, waiting to take their first cruise vacation.

"I said at one time in a speech: Cruising was all about the overfed, the almost dead, and the newlyweds, and that was it," Williams says.

But that statement was made prior to the creation of the Voyager Class ship. Williams knew the market potential was much bigger. The company felt big ship potential—with lots of activities on board, like high-production theatrical shows, ice skating rinks, and surfing experiences—would turn the ships themselves into *destinations*.

The key for Royal Caribbean was making a ship of that magnitude still feel pleasantly intimate. As they increased their knowledge on what the demands of a potential customer expected of their product, so bloomed their faith.

"I think intuitively there was a lot of belief that the design was working itself out on paper and then working itself out in the ship-yard," Williams says. "You were seeing it come together. Having been very close to customer feedback and knowing that we could replicate that experience and make it even better, even though it was on a bigger ship, all added to the confidence that this was probably going to work."

The gamble paid off.

"We started bringing more and more first-timers into the cruise experience than ever before," Williams says. "It just got a life of its own; it really did."

Today, Royal Caribbean Cruises has revenues just shy of $9 billion and employs 66,000 people.[12] The big picture is that the company had the courage to address its product fears head-on with knowledge, faith, and action. They transformed their cruise ships and, by doing so, changed the trajectory of an entire industry.

When probed on the landscape of business today, the now retired Williams believes one of the largest problems in corporate America is a lack of courage, largely because there's a deficit when it comes to courageous leaders.

"We have a whole plethora of safe leaders. They're not challenging; they're not pushing the boundaries of where they can go with that company," he says. "Where are you willing to challenge business models? What are you willing to walk up to and look over and see what's down on that side of that cliff there?"

What's in the way is the way.

SERVICE FEARS

Imagine you just bought a beautiful house in a gated community. At first, your gorgeous home is surrounded by a handful of other impressive neighborhood chateaus that are just as nice. But over time, you start to notice that many of the other houses being built near your property are not up to the same standard. And while you work hard to keep your property looking pristine, your neighbors haven't exactly kept up with the renovating times.

This was the predicament facing premium content provider HBO with satellite and cable television. Thanks to streaming via the Internet, cable TV was not the neighborhood it used to be.

Nowadays, we have access to a panoply of content options through branded entertainment choices like Netflix, Amazon Prime, Apple, Hulu, and YouTube. HBO recognized the hard decision it needed to make regarding its service fear. Instead of being totally dependent on the cable bundle, it made the difficult yet innovative move to jump the cable pay wall with the creation of its HBO Now service.

"It is time to remove all barriers to those who want HBO," chairman and CEO Richard Plepler stated at a 2015 press conference. He also noted that HBO would be releasing a "stand-alone, over-the-top" service for the ever-growing community of cord cutters.[13]

It's not easy to get a divorce from your long-lasting collaborator cable television. Time Warner made just under $5 billion in revenue in 2015 from its lucrative HBO relationship. Although HBO expanded its audience, it did not stop providing its service through cable. The HBO Go streaming app is also available to those who pay for an HBO cable subscription. But after so many years on cable, HBO is addressing its fears head-on and doing what it believes is best for business. With no cable or satellite subscription needed to watch HBO Now (which at the time of writing this book could be added for $15 a month), it's a game of command and control that allows HBO to go after the 80 million homes currently without access.

From a service fear standpoint, HBO is an excellent example of a service provider that is being courageous and striving to make the right moves to stay ahead of potential business pitfalls.

Providing a service for cord cutters and evolving its services are just a few ways HBO showed it could keep its house in that gated community and pick up an apartment in the big digital city.

PERCEPTION FEARS

Imagine that you are the chair of the board of family owned Black & Decker. Just about every American in the country knows your company by name. You have a well-earned reputation for quality and durability with a brand strength rating ranked near the top with Coca-Cola, Walt Disney, and NBC. You sell superior products and have an exemplary, top-notch sales force.

So imagine your surprise when a case started being made to abolish the Black & Decker name entirely from the professional tradesman category.[14] Did I mention that 98 percent of tradespeople are familiar with your high-quality brand?

So what's the problem? The popcorn maker.

Tradesmen wouldn't be caught dead on a construction site lugging around the same brand that made the toaster and popcorn maker their spouses regularly use at home.

So even though the Black & Decker tools remained a superior product, a majority of rough-and-tumble types were afraid to arrive at a job in fear of being mocked by their peers.

We have drilled squarely into a perception fear.

Black & Decker knew it couldn't overcome the anti-advocacy that was happening on construction sites prior to 1992. Even with a high-quality power brand to match its high-quality power products, the company's business in the professional trade segment was floundering.

To overcome this perception, Black & Decker decided on an almost unthinkable, yet calculated and courageous option.

Already the owners of the brand DeWalt, a company respected by tradesmen for the radial arm saws it produced, Black & Decker reimagined the industrial power tools space by bringing DeWalt into the category, in effect replacing *itself*.

The internal team had gathered deep knowledge wherever it could that confirmed this decision. They talked at length with industrial tradesmen about what they needed and didn't want on construction sites. The more the team learned, the more it believed it could credibly and successfully introduce DeWalt to tradesmen.

With a perception fear like no other, Black & Decker began to take itself out of the trade game for good. Many felt that DeWalt, as an American brand, could play well on construction sites across the country and had a shot to be an instant hit that could hammer down the sales of Japanese leader Makita.

They were right. Dropping the Black & Decker name for DeWalt led to a consistent rise in sales, jumping from $60 million in 1992 to an astronomical $1 billion in 1999.

Black & Decker, with the help of DeWalt, has bulldozed its Japanese competitor ever since.

PERSONAL FEARS

"We pay a heavy price for our fear of failure," noted John W. Gardner, who won the Presidential Medal of Freedom serving under President Lyndon Johnson as the US Secretary of Health, Education, and Welfare. "It is a powerful obstacle to growth."[15]

There is one more kind of fear everyone deals with on a daily basis: fear of failure. Nobody wants to fail. We are so afraid to fail that it often means we won't even take the necessary steps to try to succeed.

The question is what are we so afraid of?

And why are we so terrified in the first place?

NeuroGym CEO John Assaraf shares, "I can ask somebody, 'What are you afraid of?' They may say, 'I'm afraid of public speaking.' No, you're not. You're afraid of being ashamed, embarrassed, or ridiculed."[16]

Assaraf believes these personal fears are often tied to something that occurred during our childhood, and those neural patterns are still found deep within your unconscious brain, affecting your daily behavior and causing you to be afraid.

He suggests that about 5 percent of folks can make some progress fighting their way out of this. The remaining 95 percent don't have the awareness or training to beat the freeze or flight portion of their nervous system—which, as we've learned, is a natural, automatic response for most.

When University of Colorado clinical psychologist Emily Cox-Martin looks at personal fear, she defines it as anything that over activates the sympathetic nervous system.[17] This type of inner fear is triggered if and when your sympathetic nervous system stimulates your body's fight-or-flight response. Or, in laymen's terms, when something important to you—something that you truly value—is threatened, your personal fear is on the rise.

Many of us, especially those reading this book, value being successful in our careers. Unfortunately, the stressful nature of business causes us to doubt ourselves and often keeps us up at night. Fender chief marketing officer Evan Jones confesses, "Some nights I sleep great, and some nights I'm up at 3:00 a.m."[18]

We have good days. We have bad days. We relish big wins. We suffer crash and burn failures. And we speculate about it all. We dream about what life will be like during all types of future scenarios—the promotions, the failures, and even the ugly terminations. We make up scenarios about what could happen in our heads rather than staying focused on the moment and activating courage in real time.

The good news is courage is a team game. Therefore, combating fear, assuming you've rallied your Believers, can be, too.

○━☆

One way to combat fear is by having your Believership assign a mini team, an experimental task force (ETF), to a fear or blind spot.

Where most of your company remains ground soldiers, the ETF gets the time, space, and budget to tackle big problems that could pop up in the future. They are focused on their mission and empowered to unearth or recommend innovative, revenue-generating opportunities before your competitors do. Wherever you need courage the most is where you should employ your ETF.

What makes a good task force member?

OUR 4 T'S COME INTO PLAY HERE:

- **Talent**: Top players working with other top players.

- **Team**: A diverse unit in a safe, trusting environment.

- **Tenacity**: Team persistence plus resilience to pursue the mission.

- **Training**: Hours of ingrained repetition as practice makes courage.

This experimental task force acts as your company's "special forces." It is composed of your best talent across a wide range of titles and disciplines. These peer-to-peer players can strip away hierarchy for the greater good of getting to the root of a company's fear.

Just like your Believership should be limited in number, your ETF should follow that same principle. Amazon has a "two-pizza rule" it abides by. If the team has to be fed by more than two pizzas, the team on the project is too big.

Better recommendations can be made when small groups can act as the checks and balances team for the organization. An ETF consists of a blend of people who can best recommend future actions and usually doesn't include the most senior leaders, who are far away from the reality of the day-to-day job. The task force members are not tainted by past hurdles and can speak freely without feeling any repercussions from the top because the Believership trusts them to report back on the truths they uncover.

This is just one way the Believers at your company can smartly identify your industry fears, product fears, service fears, perception fears, and the realities of your personal fears head-on.

High-pressure situations give us the opportunity to learn. Fear is the ultimate filter we must go through before we can begin to make calculated courageous decisions. The more you address those fears the weaker those fears should become.

> Remember, fear is ordinary. It's as normal
> as the air we breathe.

I have fears. You have fears. Our largest competitor has fears. Every person at every business has fear. But our own fears are intensified because our own livelihood is at stake. Once we realize this, we can begin to normalize how we channel our courage to address these masterful problems. This makes fear less *fearful*. It allows us to start delivering on calculated, bold solutions that shrink down even the most pressing issues.

> Don't steer clear of the fear: Find it.
> Face it. Shrink it. Then replace it.

Once we do so, we can courageously begin to transform our organizations. And how do we do that?

By pinpointing our meaningful reason for existing.

IDENTIFY FEARS
WORKSHEET

EVERY BUSINESS HAS fears, and yours does too. There are four different types of fears to identify: Industry Fears, Product Fears, Service Fears, and Perception Fears. To arrive at a courageous decision, you first must properly identify what your business fears are and how you react to them.

1. **Do you believe the Believership has properly pinpointed the most important business fears to shrink? Identify your company's three largest fears.**

   Are you talking about fears openly with your team? Have you landed on the right fears to address? With your team, identify and prioritize the three largest fears throughout the organization. Try to pinpoint if the fear your company is facing is an Industry Fear, a Product/Service Fear, or a Perception Fear.

   a.

   b.

   c.

2. **Have you used any available resources looking for an industry blind spot? Have you created an experimental task force?**

Often, it's not what you see, it's what has yet to make itself known that can take your business down. Assemble an experimental task force (ETF) to identify and take down industry blind spots. List four to six people who should be on your ETF. Consider a wide range of employees from all levels to round out this team. As a refresher, give the ETF time, space, and a budget to help form recommendations to eliminate future threats to your business.

a.

b.

c.

d.

e.

f.

3. **Today's fears may look different than a fear that's a decade away. Run the exercise on what a fear could look like in three, five, or ten years.**

Whether it's a fear that's right in front of you, or one that could be five years out, list your fears according to different timeframes. For example, what fears do you have now? What fears do you think you'll face in three years? Five years? A decade? Smoking out these potential fears now, even if they're wrong, helps drum up conversations to best prepare to thrive tomorrow.

    a.

    b.

    c.

    d.

    e.

4. **How will you courageously address each of these fears and threats head-on? Prioritize one or two ways to take on each fear listed.**

What solutions will you recommend to address and combat each of the listed fears head-on? When you start to successfully shrink these fears, you may end up on another competitor's fear list. Better to be on their list than them on yours!

    a.

    b.

    c.

    d.

    e.

5. **Have the honest conversation with yourself. What personal fears do you have regarding your current organization? When personal fears creep in, where can you turn to address them? List three personal fears you have and list three colleagues you can talk to.**

Courage is a team game. Who else on your team, on the Believership, or on your ETF can you go to with personal fears that won't make you feel exposed? Write out three personal fears you're feeling and list three office mates you can talk to about these types of concerns.

a.

b.

c.

COMMIT TO A PURPOSE

"I am increasingly concerned about SpaceX going public before the Mars transport system is in place. Creating the technology needed to establish life on Mars is and always has been the fundamental goal of SpaceX. If being a public company diminishes that likelihood, then we should not do so until Mars is secure."
—Elon Musk, 2013 company-wide email[1]

ELON MUSK IS a man on a mission.

That mission, when it comes to SpaceX, is singularly focused: human life on Mars.

If you work at SpaceX, it's crystal clear what you signed up for. You are all-in, completely committed to this cause.

> As for you, do you partake in a job, a career, or a calling? Which would be most fulfilling?

Ashlee Vance wrote about the purpose-driven pioneer in his book *Elon Musk: Tesla, SpaceX, and the Quest for a Fantastic Future,* "What

Musk has developed that so many of the entrepreneurs in Silicon Valley lack is a meaningful worldview. While the 'putting man on Mars' talk can strike some people as loopy, it gave Musk a unique rallying cry for his companies."[2]

As a brand, you matter if you put in the effort to matter. You're special if you believe what you're offering can be perceived as authentic and valuable. Finding that genuine, unique gift you can offer the world, whether you're a being or a brand, is how you identify, declare, and live out your purpose.

Facebook owns a whopping 50 minutes of its users' days. Inside Facebook is the mission statement: "Bring the world closer together."[3] The power of connection is its committed purpose. It's the idea of freedom—making the world more accessible, open, and connected.

With the Purpose Hotel, founder Jeremy Cowart is determined to harmoniously shape a hotel that gives back to children and charities. He intends to build the hotel in Nashville, and he's midway through his purpose-driven plan to raise funds and awareness, including a successful Kickstarter campaign. By booking a room, guests would be supporting sustainable furnishings and sponsoring a child's education. Human trafficking survivors would have woven your bed sheets while your checkout bill would detail whom you are helping with your stay. The goal is to create a hotel experience that's perpetually purposeful.[4]

As another example, CVS Pharmacy took action and quit selling tobacco products in 2014, sacrificing a whopping $2 billion in annual sales. The elimination of tobacco products propelled CVS back in line with its purpose: *helping you on your path to better health*. Not only was this the right thing for CVS to do, but it was also rewarded with a soaring stock price that surged 55 percent in the year following the bold announcement.[5]

Declaring a purpose isn't something for a company's chief sustainability officer to handle as a side project. It isn't made up by marketing.

Today, a company's purpose is its authentic reason for existing. It should articulate not only how it's bettering the lives of its customers but also how it's bettering their worlds.

As the Values Arrow illustrates, your purpose should be inspired by and start with your core values and then come to life in your offerings, future products, organization, brand, board, and marketing—a shot straight through every area of your business. A good purpose should be the reason people continue to work for you. It's why your staff remains confident in your company.

To pick a purpose is to make a choice. What is your brand willing to commit to *or* sacrifice to make sure your purpose succeeds?

Zappos believes it's in the happiness business. It prides itself on being a great customer service-oriented company that happens to sell shoes. Crayola sets out to assist parents and teachers to inspire colorful, creative children. Dove is purposefully focused on making women feel *more* beautiful rather than simply making more women feel beautiful. Amazon is customer-obsessed, not competitor-obsessed.

These are what my old colleague and inspirational author Simon Sinek has coined the "why" statement for companies.[6] The more virtuous a company's purpose is, the easier it is to commit to it. And this doesn't just apply to prospects or customers. You also have to give your employees a reason to stick around.

> Today, the pathway to success is not just
> knowing your why. You have to put a rally
> cry in your why.

Nathan Smith, my former colleague and current head of brand connections at Hustle LA, believes that "a rally cry by definition incites advocacy and, if executed correctly, can create a movement that leads to demonstrative change versus incremental change."[7]

The advocates you need first are the ones within your own walls. A rally cry in your why unites and ignites your internal Believers. It motivates internal staff as much as external prospects.

To uncover, discover, and create one big "rally cry in your why" purpose, your brand

1. Must Be Truthful.

2. Must Be Purposeful.

3. Must Be Emotional.

4. Must Be Differential.

MUST BE TRUTHFUL

Contrary to popular belief, "the truth hurts" is a fallacy. In fact, the opposite is true. The truth *helps*.

Often, it's by delivering the truth and nothing but the truth to the public that makes you realize this. And this truth can't be just any truth but instead a bit of uncovered, startling information that when shared with the public surprises them and makes them notice you. Bringing that uniquely genuine truth to the surface by unearthing something that we all feel but had yet to be articulated is what makes a great purpose.

This was the case with Unilever-owned detergent brand Persil, which recognized that children were only spending an average of one hour of playtime outside per day.[8]

Persil chose to shine a light on this sad reality through a documentary-style two-minute short film shot in a location where folks are forcefully locked up for 22 hours at a time: a maximum-security prison in the middle of Indiana's cornfield country. These convicts know how precious outside time truly is, as most of them are confined inside most of the day. When asked to ponder what life behind bars would be like if that outdoor freedom time *was cut in half,* the prisoners are visibly shaken.

In this short, Persil communicates to the prisoners that most children these days are spending roughly the same amount of time playing outside. They are startled to hear this.

What Persil wisely chose to exclude from the film was a scene of spinning penitentiary clothes inside a larger-than-life washing machine or an extreme close-up product shot of a blue Persil detergent bottle. Instead, it focused on its message: its call *for* action and a "rally cry in their why" message of "Free the Kids."

Persil's film brought a truth to the forefront. It then started a conversation, and it drove parents to the microsite dirtisgood.com in an effort to encourage more kids to get outside and play.

When looking for your truthful purpose, don't be afraid to start with whatever imperfections your brand may have. Embracing the truth, even when it might at first be a negative, can be flipped into a positive. Go back to what we learned from Domino's. A brand that accepts its freckles can become an approachable, endearing company that people rally behind.

With a truthful purpose at the center of your message, consumers will see your marketing not as a necessary evil but as a necessary good.

MUST BE PURPOSEFUL

What could be more purposeful than a company that nudges other companies to be *more purposeful?*

That's the innovative path that Jay Coen Gilbert and his two closest friends went down after selling their athletic footwear and apparel giant AND 1. They pivoted from being one of basketball's most dominant forces to being one of the globe's most harmonious, good-for-the-world businesses.

Gilbert remembers watching his apparel company swiftly plummet south just months after the buyout by the negligent new leadership.

Reminiscing about that disenchanting time, Gilbert recalls, "Any of the good stuff that we had built into the company in terms of supplier relationships or great work environment, culturally, were completely stripped out. That's one of the reasons why we were looking for a way to build socially responsible businesses and help them be built to last through different phases of a company's lifetime."[9]

Hence the ambitious task by Bart Houlihan, Andrew Kassoy, and Jay Coen Gilbert of powering a purpose-centric and hopeful global movement called B Lab.

B Lab, responsible for crafting and administering the comprehensive certification process behind B Corp (Benefits Corporation), is now a decade old and filled with more than 2,500 purpose-driven companies worldwide.

This collective, which meets the rigid standards of good conscience performance, accountability, and transparency, includes socially stellar companies like Ben & Jerry's, Method, Unilever, and Patagonia.

According to Patagonia CEO Rose Marcario, "The B Corp movement is one of the most important of our lifetime, built on the simple fact that business impacts and serves more than just shareholders. It has an equal responsibility to the community and to the planet."[10]

Gilbert suggests he's trying to simultaneously build and activate that "good for the world, good for business" community in unison. It's been the path less traveled. What he and his partners were doing was truly innovative, so they had fewer examples to turn to for how to build this kind of business effectively.

He readily admits his team is colliding against cultural norms. "It's very easy to get locked in the business cage jail and only have to justify your decisions based upon a short-term ROI,"[11] he says.

Gilbert is alluding to a challenging nemesis that he believes many businesses face today: irresponsibility.

> Meaningful aspirations often shine a light on an
> enemy and work hard to bring that enemy down.

Declaring an enemy draws a clear line in the sand, asking all of those around you "Are you with us or against us?" There's excitement, suspense, and a reason to stick around: to see if you can fulfill the mission of conquering this foe. To know your enemy is to know what you stand for.

B Lab sees its clear enemy to be irresponsible business leaders running irresponsible businesses. Says Gilbert, "Business can't just be about the bottom line."

The bigger the agreed-upon enemy is, the bigger the potential rallying movement against it will be. One swift way to focus your team is to show them the injustice of this chosen enemy. Popular enemies include greed, power, deceit, constraint, evil, and inaction.

B Lab instigates business leaders to ask themselves the hard questions: Are you a responsible business or an irresponsible business?

Are you a force for good or a force for evil?

And it takes courage to thwart a nemesis of this magnitude.

Gilbert points out that "the courageous path is not the easiest path to getting a decision made or meeting a quarterly number. When courage is talked about in our circle, it's usually when a CEO or managing partner of an investment firm says, 'I'd like to do this, but I don't know if I can.' A lot of the time, there's a lack of courage."

But this company is dedicated to its mission. B Lab has a company declaration that valiantly professes, "We envision a global economy that uses business as a force for good."

It is this magnetic rallying cry that unites its business community and attracts, engages, and makes Believers out of its employees. It can inspire others to join what B Lab calls, "the responsible business movement."

> This higher purpose acts as more than a mere call to action. Rather, it's a call **for** action.

A call *for* action, not simply a call *to* action, is a critical component one needs as part of a successful purpose. A call for action gives your staff a meaningful reason to stick around and make good on the mission.

At my special forces consultancy Courageous, the "rally cry in our why" purpose is to help our clients *liberate with courage.* What we've noticed is that 95 percent of companies are stuck in preservation mode, and only 5 percent are in liberation mode. This leads to our call for action: to help our clients choose courage rather than end up in the abyss of business normalcy.

MUST BE EMOTIONAL

Have you ever tried to figure out what the chemicals in many household cleaning products actually are? Difficult to pronounce ingredients like disodium distyrylbiphenyl disulfonate, myristamine oxide, or my personal favorite, sodium C10-16 alkylbenzene sulfonate, belong in spelling bees not in our household cleaning products.

If you ever wondered what these super-syllabic words were or questioned why you need to slip on those protective yellow rubber gloves when cleaning your home, you are not alone.

These questions are what inspired Eric Ryan and childhood friend

Adam Lowry to launch eco-friendly soap company Method into action in 2001. An ex-strategic planner at an advertising agency, Ryan was convinced that "there's no such thing as low-interest categories, just low-interest brands."[12]

So Ryan and his partner set out to create and stand for something bigger than the usual artificial disinfectant products that were currently cleaning up at the cash register. Ryan believed they could create a paradigm shift within this chemically saturated category. The goal? Create an emotional connection where there wasn't one before.

Ryan and Lowry started by gathering data on their identified target of "progressive domestics." They felt the audience would pay more for a higher-quality product that was presented impressively through its attractive packaging design.

When they finally landed on their "rally cry in their why" purpose, they knew it was perfect for them: *The People Against Dirty.*

It was a direct hit against companies using hazardous materials, and the perfect mantra for a passionate company that aspired to make something good for human health, as well as for animal health. (Method does not test on animals.)

"It was a cultural shift for the consumer," Ryan says. "We were taking a really boring category and making it a bit sexy. Everyone else in our category was trying to win on science; we were trying to win on people."

And they did.

Tapping into an emotional purpose resonated with those passionate people who were "against dirty." Those most fervently aligned joined the Method tribe and shared their feelings with their networks through word of mouth and social channels. All at no extra cost to the brand.

What previous experience did Ryan and Lowry have in the category? None. They followed their faith and believed they could fill a void. They had a grasp on the desires of a younger generation and the conviction to continue to pursue what others doubted.

Method can now be found in the aisles of Target all over America. The company generates gross revenues north of $100 million annually.[13]

This is emotion at work.

MUST BE DIFFERENTIAL

If you have landed on a truthful, unique, and emotional purpose, but someone else has already declared that reason for existing, you have to move on to another purpose.

When choosing a purpose, being different is what will set you apart. How high your ceiling extends depends on that.

Southwest evolved its purpose, summing it up in one authentic differentiator not found with any other airline. They call it Transfarency.

We have come to expect transparency from Southwest that is not found at other airlines. This describes the way Southwest presents itself as well as its "bags fly free" pricing policy. That transparent, approachable, and down-to-earth openness sums up what makes Southwest different. And the airline owns it.

Different is also better when it comes to growth. Online advertising resource Kantar Millward Brown reported: "Brands that are felt to be positively unique and setting trends in their category have grown much more dramatically—by an average of 124 percent. Those that have been less successful in being different have grown by 24 percent."[14]

Remember, your purpose can't just be different for the sake of being different. It must still be truthful, purposeful, and emotional.

Delivering on being different is what will set you apart.

TRUTHFUL + PURPOSEFUL + EMOTIONAL + DIFFERENTIAL = WORTHY, COMMITTED PURPOSE

When you add truth, purpose, emotion, and uniqueness together, you get a motivational purpose to which your company can commit. Companies that choose their purpose wisely are handsomely rewarded for doing so.

Developed by *Grow* author Jim Stengel, the Stengel 50 shows a connection between brands differentiating themselves by serving a higher purpose and lucrative returns delivered back to stakeholders. Monitoring the financial performance of these companies over a 10-year period, the Stengel 50 was 400 percent more profitable than an investment in the S&P 500.[15]

Peter Walshe, global BrandZ strategy director at Kantar Millward Brown, found similar positive results for purpose-driven companies. In an article, Walshe reported that brands with a strong purpose and high advertising strength grew 168 percent, while brands with a weak purpose but high advertising strength only grew 27 percent.[16]

It's important to secure a purpose that you believe can sustain the test of time. It's critical that brands choose a broad enough purpose that allows them to stretch their offerings as they evolve into the future. I call this *Purpose Elasticity.*

As your company creates proactive products or offerings to keep it relevantly speeding forward, your purpose should be able to stretch to cover any new potential revenue stream you put into the market.

Committing to a purpose means injecting an authentic rally cry in your why. Internally, this keeps your Believers vested and retained, eager to see if the team can fulfill the meaningful mission as a unit.

Look to inject a call *for* action, which always tops a call *to* action. Having a call for action, and an identified enemy to combat, motivates the masses and gives Believers a reason to become a part of your team.

This is asking people to decide between what you stand for and what you won't put up with.

The clearer this higher-calling purpose is, the easier it'll be to execute company-wide and beyond.

Which brings us to the here and now.

We've finally arrived at go time.

Everything you just learned is all for naught if we don't put what we learned into action.

COMMIT TO A PURPOSE WORKSHEET

A POWERFUL PURPOSE is so much more than words. Having an authentic cause drives conviction and keeps your staff motivated to come to work, even on those tough days. It becomes ingrained in your company culture. It could permeate outside the walls of your organization and transform a one-time purchaser into a beloved customer and advocate.

1. **Have you declared your company's purpose? Write it down now.**

   Remember, a purpose should touch all four quadrants: truthful, emotional, purposeful, and differential. Write down your authentic cause for being. If it hasn't been fulfilled yet, so long as it's truly motivating (See: SpaceX), that's OK. If it's not known yet, write down three potential purposes and how they correspond to the four quadrants.

   a.

2. **Who is your company's enemy?**

   When it comes to landing on your purpose, it's often easier to start by identifying your enemy. The enemy can be symbolic like greed, lack of access, or injustice. List your potential enemy and remember there is no gray area! There should be a clear line making it easy for people to decide if they are with you or against you (for example, Method's "The People Against Dirty"). If there are several enemies, prioritize them by how powerfully you are called to defeat them.

    a.

3. **What is your call *for* action?**

    How are you igniting a movement? A call to action doesn't hold the gravitas of a call for action. A call for action instigates your community and moves them to participate. What's your call for action outside of customers purchasing your product?

    a.

4. **Review your answers. Do your listed purpose(s), enemy, and call for action make Believers want to stick around? Are they meaningful enough to break through the noise to catch the eye of advocates? If not, go bigger! List three "rally cry in your why" purposes to explore.**

    Do you have your courageous "rally cry in your why"? Is it powerful enough to galvanize your staff and energize your customer base? Why or why not? Not there yet? Amp up your answer! Jot down three lofty purposes that are meaningful enough to pursue and commit to.

    a.

    b.

    c.

EXECUTE YOUR ACTION

I'M AN ACTION guy. That's not news to those who know me. I'm the guy at restaurants who's ready to order first, and if others are being indecisive, I will order appetizers for the table. And if you let me run the show at a sushi meal, you won't be disappointed.

On a business front, I've spent almost two decades crafting persuasive messages that relevantly shape my clients' stories for their potential customers. I've tackled complicated communication problems on behalf of brands since the day I entered the New York City workforce. Cracking messy marketing mazes with clarity is where I'm most skilled, and it's where my passion lies.

This is why, of the five sections of the Central Courage System, I am breaking code to admit the *E* in P.R.I.C.E. is my favorite: execute.

So here we are.

You now know what you stand for. You have rallied like-minded, aligned Believers. You've identified a fearful threat you simply can't let run unchecked. You've committed to a worthy purpose. Now, it's time to act.

Whether that action is the creation of a new product or service or preparing a new consumer-facing story, once you've gathered your knowledge and built up enough faith, then it's time to Execute Your Action.

There are two distinct paths you will find your teams executing on:

- A New Offering
- A New Message

A NEW OFFERING

To paraphrase Charles Darwin, "It is not the strongest species that survive, nor the most intelligent, but the ones most responsive to change."[1]

Change is constant in any evolving organization. In fact, change is constant in life in general.

Companies that succeed use their elastic purpose to create new products that keep them changing and relevant. Their purpose must be able to stretch to cover any potential new revenue stream they put into the market.

The ultimate goal is to put your company in a position to create new products or services that can one day be an industry fear to the competitors in your category.

Now retired president of Royal Caribbean Jack Williams supports this notion. Williams recalls their ambitious quest to become what he calls a "Category One" brand. Category One brands do everything in their power to become a category of one. A Category One brand, in Williams' eyes, included companies like Southwest or Cirque du Soleil.

"If you want to have that same kind of experience again, provided by a Cirque du Soleil show, you have to go back to Cirque du Soleil. Nobody else does that,"[2] he says.

Williams notes that focusing his team on becoming a Category One brand was not simply about transforming the business. Rather, it was a calculated, conscious attempt discussed regularly by his team to make their competition *irrelevant.*

Williams believes that after they built the larger Voyager Class ships they achieved Category One status. "Once you went on that ship, if you wanted that experience again, there was nowhere else to go," he says. "You had to go back there. That is a very powerful place to be."

The Voyager Class ship catapulted Royal Caribbean into that exclusive one-of-a-kind class for quite some time. Williams believes it truly helped the company become a dominant force in every aspect of its business for a long time.

"That's the difference between talking about being a relevant company versus how do I make my competition irrelevant," he says. "You can do one of the two, but if you can get your business to a Category One and you create a powerful mind-set, watch out, you're going to go a long, long way."

So how do you make the time—which we don't have enough of— to properly create innovative offerings that propel your company into relevancy while simultaneously making your competition irrelevant? This, again, can be a job for an experimental task force (ETF).

According to Google vice president and mobile expert Jason Spero, "There's a lot of talk about Silicon Valley rewarding failure, but I think that one of the ways we help our big customers get past that is to take a small percentage of the budget or a small percentage of your team and let them perform the experiments so that we limit our risk."[3]

As for Google's quest to mitigate its risk, Spero suggests the king of search is conducting its own experiments to tackle business fears directly. Spero states, "We've continued to spend a very significant percentage on research and development, and we've told Wall Street that's what we're going to do. I think that does take courage. I don't want us to back down from that."

Spero admits this type of lean-forward investing is entrenched in the culture of Google. And, yes, it helps when you have a surplus of cash to work on future company offerings, such as artificial intelligence, virtual reality, wearables, or the Cloud. For companies tighter on cash, it becomes more difficult—and it may take more courage.

Spero has advice for any Believership team trying to transform their company to compete in a mobile-heavy world. "If I were a CMO or a CEO at one of these companies trying to adapt, I would take 5 percent of my budget, and I would take some of my smartest, most mobile-savvy people, and I would say, 'You have a year to build me a system that I could move half my budget to. Here's 5 percent of the budget; use it to conduct the needed experiments.'"

The goal of the Believership would then be to provide that ETF with enough air cover to construct, carry out, and support the experiment. What comes back may not always be optimal. But the alternative is sticking with your current business model, and as we've already discussed, one of the truths of the Business Apocalypse is what got you here won't keep you here.

This brings us to a principle inspired by our military: cover and move.

COVER AND MOVE

The Navy SEALs have a core executional principle known as cover and move. In this context, it's covering your teammates before they move as a unit to the next location.

In business terms, cover and move is one way you can think about testing how elastic your purpose truly is. You have to "cover" your current products while you work to "move" toward your next revenue stream or innovation, all while remaining true to your existing purpose.

Amazon's cover used to be a surplus of offerings delivered directly to users' doorsteps. Now, Amazon has made a move with the introduction of Echo. Better known as Alexa, the ultimate intelligent in-home utility, Echo can play a song for your children at your request. It can add grocery items to your shopping list on your command.

Amazon first satisfied you with free two-day shipping. Now, it has moved to an in-house Internet of Things that is your personal assistant. Consulting giant Gartner predicts that 30 percent of all searches will be voice-activated by 2020.[4] And who is perfectly nestled inside your home already? Amazon.

Fender isn't just sticking to its "cover" of handcrafted guitars. It's working on developing uncharted territory in a "move" to teach novice guitar players how to play through digital learning experiences including teaching players how to jam through Fender Play. They're doing so in song-based tutorials that *Fast Company* writes, "puts YouTube lessons to shame."[5]

These cover-and-move moments attempt to maximize future revenues by covering current offerings before moving on to developing new products or services—all under one elastic, worthy purpose.

So, when it comes to creating a potential new offering, identify a business fear or industry blind spot. You can attack this at a senior level off-site much like Merck did with its "What could kill the company?" exercise. Or you can create an internal ETF to tackle this situation.

While the majority of your current employees act as your army, covering your existing revenue streams, this ETF is given the time, space, and budget to take on the future by recommending your potential new move.

From there, it's up to your Believership to put that new offering into action.

A NEW MESSAGE

Whether you are launching a new product or service, or evolving your brand with a worthwhile story, there are ways to rise above the noise so that your target audience can actually see and hear you.

Gaining their attention, of course, is not enough. Once you have their attention, you have to persuade.

When it comes to the power of persuasion, it's important to make something acutely clear: Your job is not to directly persuade anyone of anything. Persuasion has little to do with your witty ability to convince someone of something. Your mission, if you choose to accept it, is to give people just enough information on your product or idea that they will persuade *themselves.*

When Southwest gabs about Transfarency, you think, *Finally. Yes. That's for me. At last, an airline that gets me.*

When you think about LinkedIn, you probably don't think social media network. Instead, this thought might cross your mind: *Here's where I can stalk the fine citizens of business nation* (in a nice stalking way, of course).

Persuasion gets a bad rap.

If it's done right, persuasion doesn't have to be manipulation. It's not a used car salesman trying to get you into a 2010 Dodge Durango. Persuasion is stating your case by showing more than telling. Walking the walk tops talking the talk. Persuasion is all the stuff you do that, when it comes together, helps others arrive at their own conclusions as to why this must-have product or idea fits wonderfully into their lives.

Persuasion performed perfectly doesn't convince people to do something. The people convince themselves.

Consumers connect their own dots.

You nudge, they judge.

But the rules of the game have changed quite a bit since social media arrived. Today, the brands that are winning get that persuading isn't something a brand does on its own. It's something a person's network of coworkers, friends, and family do.

They hear about that crazed Pokémon app not from a print ad but from their morning barista at Starbucks or in a sideline conversation with that soccer dad whose name they should know by now.

A Nielsen poll of 25,000 Internet consumers showed that 90 percent of respondents "completely" or "somewhat" trust recommendations from friends or acquaintances—much higher than those who trust newspaper ads (59 percent) or online banners (33 percent).[6]

Even with this knowledge, many marketers still choose to play by the old rules of the marketing game. They don't realize they are *not* persuading, but rather, they are dissuading their audience.

As an unintentional dissuader, you are spending your company's hard-earned dollars to contribute to this careless but stoppable act.

Every day, thousands of brands *think* they are doing the right thing. Unbeknownst to many, they are just adding to the marketing junkyard.

Bad advertising is a nuisance. It works against you.

You are only as good as the message you create. Once crafted, the game quickly turns to *advocacy*.

Like a rock skipping across the pond, your job is to implement a story that gets influential advocates to buy in and share your message with their networks.

When it comes to nailing down an advocate-worthy story, the momentum-making content must be

- **Authentic**: Original content continues to be difficult for companies to execute. It shouldn't be! The resources at your disposal are endless. Shift your thinking away from the traditional, and consider yourself as a media conglomerate. Look to make original content like documentaries, live experiential events, or digital games. You could even start charity foundations, create password-protected online music concerts, or incubate an on-brand web series. If people call your marketing "marketing," you probably missed the mark.

- **Aspirational**: Ideas that make their way to the front of the line compel us to participate. Those ideas usually stand for something. They are not trying to be all things to all people. Aspirational ideas are purposeful ideas. They captivate and attract us.

- **Amazing**: It's not easy to amaze. Something is considered amazing because it is new and has never been done before. When you see something that is amazing, you want to be the first to share that magic with your friends or family so they will be amazed, too. Ultimately, when you amaze, you persuade. When you successfully persuade, you have created an advocate.

The best advertising is no longer recognized as advertising. It's now called *content*. With so many accessible media vehicles, you don't have to tell your story all at once. You can craft cliffhangers and leave clues all over the Internet that point the story to different locations, microsites, and channels. Advertising is alive and well; it just looks a lot different than it used to.

The "best of" is being shared by persuaded, inspired advocates who are still amazed by your story. And we need these advocates for our stories to work.

When it comes to powering new messages, consider making these four P's a part of your purposeful marketing programs:

- Point of View
- Precision
- Passion
- Promoters

Point of View

Say you want to open a state-of-the-art San Diego brewery equipped with a full-service restaurant. Would you want your location to be in an up-and-coming downtown metropolis that's a perpetual revolving door to hundreds of thousands of convention visitors? Or would you choose a location perfectly nestled just blocks from the beach where millions of vacationers come annually to unwind, relax, and imbibe on a regular basis?

How about neither? What if your location were more remote? And then how would you let people know about you?

Would you take out a full-page ad in the city newspaper where you'd scream from the mountaintops in big, bold type the grand opening of your new brew establishment? Or would you release a series of catchy radio jingles over the airwaves letting people discover that you have finally arrived?

Once again, how about none of the above? The owners of fiercely independent Stone Brewing eschewed those traditional options when they opened the now two-decade-old, cutting-edge brewery (and then later with their now 10-year-old restaurant).

Twenty years later, you'll still find zero billboards featuring their name above the nearby highways. No two-for-one-special airplane banners above San Diego's sprawling beaches. No crafty beer television commercials airing during sports broadcasts. In fact, you won't even find a sports broadcast on a TV in Stone's bar area because you won't find a single TV on the property.

If there's no TV in the bar, then it's clearly not a sports bar. And if it's not a sports bar, then what is it?

Cofounder, executive chair, and Chief Belief Officer Greg Koch, who has been rightfully given the nickname Beer Jesus, emphatically considers Stone Brewing a destination. In fact, Stone Brewing is the third most popular destination in San Diego's North County—after the San Diego Zoo Safari Park and LEGOLAND.[7]

"When we built our brewery here, it was out of the way and hard to find, with no sign on the building," Koch says. "We had a complete ban on high-fructose corn syrup, which means no major brand sodas and no major brand ketchups and condiments that have that junk in it. We had no major brand beers, no TVs, and no french fries or burgers."[8]

Koch readily admits they did all these things you *shouldn't* do. What they did was provide an overly eclectic menu full of expensive items and a steadfast focus on all organic ingredients. "All these elements added up to doing it absolutely the wrong way by any well-reasoned, educated restaurant industry person," he says.

And they did not take part in a single traditional advertisement.

This is advocacy at its finest. Word of mouth and social media are how you find out just how authentic, aspirational, and amazing Stone Brewing truly is. In turn, Stone Brewing gets the exact customer it wants: an independent brew lover choosing an independent brewery.

With Stone Brewing being committed to its philosophy that advertising is not the answer, Koch knows that when he talks about never advertising, that in and of itself becomes his advertisement. He enjoys being able to use that strategy as part of his unapologetic, poignant point of view.

He has seen the fruits of that strategy transfer from one potential new customer to the next—enough that people are willing to drive 45 minutes north of downtown San Diego and a half hour east of any beach just to experience Stone's year-round IPAs and sensational seasonal stouts.

Over the years, Koch and partners have been wooed for purchase by many of the world's biggest beer manufacturers. Every time, Koch has turned them down.

Also unmovable for Koch was any sort of compromise on spirit, quality, or character. In his mind, he makes "real beer" and proclaims that Big Beer is his nemesis.

"Big Beer really has no brain, heart, or soul in the same way that an independent company does," he says. "They may think that I'm saying that these companies are bad or evil. No, no, no. They're just a different kind of entity."

If Big Beer is solely about commerce, then real beer must be about art. Beer Jesus profoundly pontificates: "When you think about it from the very simple terms, is beer capable of being art? Yes. Is art best when it has a point of view? Yes."

Rather than working to lock in an advocate-worthy point of view, many brand marketers settle for promoting their product's point of difference. A point of difference usually entails a handful of unique product benefits that are rarely memorable let alone shareable.

Famed strategist Seth Godin writes, "It's easy to tout your features, focus on the benefits, give proof that you are, in fact, the best solution to a problem. But proof doesn't make the sale. Of course, you believe the proof, but your audience doesn't. The very fact that you presented the proof makes it suspect."[9]

A point of difference might mean your camera battery lasts eight hours longer than your competitor's. The point of view in this instance is that you've empowered your customer with more freedom to shoot, capture, and share what's meaningful to them.

To identify your point of view is to identify your company's living, breathing creature. Usually your creature is a feeling. It's that emotional rally cry that separates you from the rest. It's a combination of whatever it is that makes you authentic, aspirational, and amazing. Outside of very few products, when was the last time you stumbled onto a product feature where the juice was worth the squeeze?

To find your point of view is to find your
brand's creature.

To win advocates, market your brand's
creature—not your product features.

Precision

Now, I'm really going to date myself here, but growing up in the '80s,
one of my all-time favorite television shows of the decade was Jim
Henson's creation *Fraggle Rock*. Fraggles were known for their care-
free silliness while the show's anti-Fraggles were the tiny-but-mighty,
work-dedicated Doozers.

While the playful Fraggles loved exploring all day, the army-like,
detail-oriented, and hard-hat wearing Doozers relished working
around the clock. If there was one thing Doozers took seriously, it was
the precise execution of their craft.

Doozers were doers.

When it comes to executing, we can learn a lot from the meticulous
Doozer. How you execute your plan is as important as the plan itself.

Thought leadership is nothing without do
leadership. **To execute with excellence is
to execute with precision.**

A poor idea wonderfully executed will outshine an exceptional idea
that didn't have the necessary polish. All that hard work goes to waste
without someone with a clear idea executing the ideas.

In the first year of i.d.e.a., we had the good fortune of represent-
ing Advanstar, a company known for putting on mass global events.

This included the International Motorcycle Show, a 13-city nationwide tour where Harley riders and bike enthusiasts could peruse the latest in motorcycles.

For our ad campaign, we sold a dream bike concept that we called "Human Motorcycles." We hired eclectic body painter Trina Merry and went to work on set bending a handful of flexible yoga gurus into complex positions. Over the course of three 18-hour days, we transformed these contorted body painted professionals into a sports bike, a speed bike, and a cruiser. We literally topped each bike off with *Speed Channel* on-air personality Erin Bates.

We truly didn't know if it was going to work, and it wasn't until we actually started the project—the testing, bending, body painting, and eventually, photographing—that we knew that the fruits of our crazy labor would magically come to fruition. The behind-the-scenes video of "Human Motorcycles" hit 1 million views in the first month alone on YouTube.

Thought leadership with subpar do leadership is the difference between a diamond idea and a graphite idea. When excellent ideas are poorly executed, the idea is nothing more than a poor idea.

Precision isn't simply about the look and feel of traditional marketing messages.

Unique precision helped Apple thoughtfully stand out with its perfected retail environment. Unique precision was on display with Method's disruptive upside-down soap packaging. Unique precision separates Tesla, with its falcon wings for doors, from almost any other car on the road.

One other point worth making here is the small difference between precision and perfection. Many believe that the quest to be perfect will leave you stagnant. You must get your message to market in an effective, timely manner. Let's not forget about that Business Apocalypse truth: You need time, but you don't have time. And keep in mind that, with so much stuff being thrown at customers, your stories have to stand strongly on their own without you there to defend it. Having that pristine precision so you stand out from the rest can make all the difference.

Passion

Have you ever tried to explain the act of being in love?

It's hard. Words fail you. Falling in love is not logical. Rather, it's a feeling that permeates your existence.

Passion, much the same way, makes you *feel*. When you are passionate about something, often words can't fully do the feeling justice. We are rarely attracted to things we aren't insanely passionate about. We certainly don't share ideas that lack emotional soul in our social channels.

As a 2015 Salesforce blog post suggested, buying decisions are based 80 percent on emotion and 20 percent on logic.[10]

The power of reason was not in play when I bought my California house. I pulled the trigger because it reminded me of my childhood. The banister and the staircase looked beautifully similar to ones I grew up with back on the East Coast. Only later did I justify this purchase as being a good buy in a good community near good schools. Deep down, I knew the *real* reason. It reminded me of a wonderful time in my life when play and exploration were my only jobs.

> Rational tells. Emotional sells.

It's the emotionally irrational that gets us to purchase something. We often can't explain it. And it doesn't need to be explained—you already made the purchase and are now looking to use that rational side of your brain to justify that decision.

Brands should follow suit.

Passionate people running passionate brands have the power to unlock passion in others. Consumers can feel when a Chief Belief Officer pours herself into a product. They can sense that Sir Richard Branson has a passion for the products he's delivering to the market.

Injecting passion into your advocacy program provokes people's irrational and emotional side. These are the kinds of things that put a little smile on our faces. It connects with something deep within our bones. Passion does a fine job of slipping right by the mind and straight into the heart.

Be the passionate, emotional choice. When the opportunity presents itself, don't be afraid to pull yourself away from the logical into that loving, passionate, and emotional arena. Be courageous and let the magic do what it's supposed to do.

Promoters

Say you've landed on a passionate point of view that has been precisely executed. While this is a reason to celebrate, it does not mean your job is complete. You have yet to crack the code on how to share that beautiful message.

You do what you do for 40 to 80 hours a week for an opportunity to make a dent in a four- to eight-second window where your marketing must work.

So how do you make the most of that short moment?

This is why influential promoters are so important.

Some write for *The New York Times*. Others influence through Instagram. Another may have a mass blog following about mass blog followings. When you win over these advocates, they can transform into your trusted promoters.

>Promoters get you accepted publicity and
>provoke participation.

Since many of us are influenced by our family, friends, and coworkers, landing our stories here first is the challenge.

Take, for instance, the largest generation in US history. Millennial shoppers spend a whopping $600 billion annually, a figure expected to reach $1.4 trillion by 2020 as reported in an Accenture study.[11]

The problem is that Millennials can *smell* sell. Millennials may have access to every screen under the sun, but that doesn't mean they are open to hearing from you. If they don't have a relationship with you already, then you have to work even harder to get your authentic, aspirational, and amazing piece of content to those who influence your network.

The good news is that Millennials are receptive to their trusted network. Author and digital marketing pioneer Jay Baer knows this all too well. Baer believes the way to build relationships in a skeptical world saturated with advertising is by simply going the extra mile when it comes to customer experience. Baer recently told me, "When you exceed customer expectations in an obvious and important way, it compels positive word of mouth. The best brands take customers and turn them into volunteer marketers."[12]

Unruly reports that 80 percent of Millennials will tune into a TV episode if someone in their network has shared a piece of content from the show with them.[13]

In the book *Contagious*, author Jonah Berger notes the average American takes part in more than 16 word-of-mouth episodes a day. He says up to 50 percent of all purchasing decisions are influenced thanks to in-person word of mouth.[14]

In this new world, we're now reliant on handing over the keys to our brands in more conversational places than ever before. We have unlimited screens to consume from, which is good news for pin-pointing your intended audience. A story that sticks with Gen Z will rarely live in the same feed or have the same outcome as it will on baby boomers. It's why your story and content needs to be perfectly crafted for the specific promoter you are trying to reach.

Content is king, context is queen, and contacts are aces

First, you need context to understand the audience, situation, timing, and competitive set. Then comes your meaningful content that will resonate with your audience. Finally, you get it to relevant promoters—those contacts who help power your message out into the world—which simultaneously promotes their personal brand to their followers.

Have you ever asked a PR professional to share their book of contacts? It won't go well if you do. That's because their contacts are the number one thing media relations people cherish.

Contacts in social media are also of ever-growing importance. And now there's an ever-growing list of companies who are in the business of connecting you with these influential micro influencers who have sway over a large number of followers.

Of course, most influencers will not push a message forward if it doesn't align with their point of view. The advocates you want to have a lasting relationship with will only put their personal brand on the line if your content is on point and mirrors their beliefs. When these promoters buy in, if it's meaningful to them, they'll willingly amplify your brand.

Narrowcasting

The idea of narrowcasting is to narrowly cast your point of view to on-board promoters, who, in turn, become walking vessels called upon to broadcast your brand's "creature" to the masses.

When you narrowcast your point of view to a passionate group, that swell of momentum is a boost of courage. When it resonates, you take off. If they don't buy in, your point of view won't go any further.

Zappos fungineer Tyler Williams is allowed to shine because the Zappos culture allows it. The culture was part of the reason Williams had the freedom to help Team Zappos stand out during the congested 2015 Black Friday-Cyber Monday long weekend. He did this not by promoting a single SKU or shoe but by partnering with Best Friends Animal Society, a national nonprofit, which helps find homes for homeless pets.

Zappos challenged its customers to adopt a pet through its heartfelt *Give Life, Get Love* Pawlidayz promotion. It started with Williams narrowcasting to passionate internal Believers. "As soon as it went live, our employees shared it 1,800 times," Williams says. "We woke up the next day and were trending number one on Facebook. We ended up trending number one for three days."[15]

Along the way, the media and celebrities who believed in the cause powered the pet adoption message as well, with big hits from Huffington Post, CBS, and FOX, while more than a hundred celebrities, including Sophia Bush, George Lopez, Jewel, and Wayne Brady shared the story with their social networks.

During a time wildly saturated with holiday discounts, Zappos' Return on Courage was rewarded for promoting something meaningful and different.

In the end, the Pawlidayz promotion received more than 200 million Twitter impressions over a 10-day period. There was a total of 275 media mentions according to the Best Friends Animal Society. More than 6,200 cats, dogs, rabbits, birds, and horses were adopted through 143 participating shelters.[16]

Narrowcast to those who align with and adore you. If someone follows your brand on social media, they are a prime candidate to become a future promoter. Make it easy for them to hit the share or forward button for the greater good of both of you.

Remember, consumers prefer to hear from their friends, families, coworkers, and social networks. Look to narrowcast your authentic, aspirational, and amazing message to selected influential promoters, and nudge those advocates to convince others to buy in, believe, and share.

EXECUTE YOUR
ACTION WORKSHEET

WHETHER IT'S TIME to create a new offer or craft a new message, the tools listed here will help you to best take action. When it comes to innovation, remember to swiftly "cover and move" with the guidance of your elastic purpose. When it's time to break through with new marketing, learn how to get your most meaningful messages into the hands of advocates by utilizing the four P's of advocacy (Passion, Precision, Promoters, and Point of View).

1. **How do you make your competition irrelevant? List three "cover and move" business innovations that could keep you relevantly ahead in business. Remember to take into consideration your newly crafted elastic purpose that allows you to propel your company forward.**

   Now comes the fun part! Think through new offerings that allow you to play offense rather than simply defending what you already have. How does this elastic purpose enable you to innovate forward? List three innovations that pave the way under your elastic purpose. Be creative!

a.

b.

c.

2. Who would make a good member of your experimental task force?

Consider this your "special forces" unit. Your ETF is responsible for innovating your tomorrow. List three to six coworkers who would thrive here. Don't limit yourself to titles, age, or current experience. Focus on who you think diversifies the ETF and brings a unique perspective to the team.

a.

b.

c.

d.

e.

f.

3. Why did you recommend these members for your experimental task force?

List one specific reason for each name you listed in Question #2.

a.

b.

c.

d.

e.

f.

4. **Deep down, do you believe you are currently persuading or dissuading?**

Overall, are you persuading or dissuading? List three things you are doing right now that persuade prospects to choose you. List three ways your company is dissuading audiences from considering you. This can include the product or offering itself, the purpose of the company, or the messaging or marketing you are putting out into the world.

a.

b.

c.

5. **On a scale of 1 to 10, how authentic, aspirational, and amazing is your current message? Why?**

Are you delivering the truth? Is your motivating rally cry or call for action coming out in your message? Do people want to share your story? Rank how authentic, aspirational, and amazing your company is on a scale of 1 to 10. Write a few sentences on why you feel the way you do.

a.

6. **Are you creating advocates? Which of the four P's of advocacy do you think you're getting right? And where are you falling short?**

   *Audit where you stand when it comes to emoting your **point of view**. How **precise** is it coming through in materials? Is there enough heart-over-head **passion** injected into the work? Enough so that influential **promoters** are willing to participate with your brand and share your message forward?*

   a.

7. **In your opinion, do your current employees advocate on behalf of your company?**

   If you had to hypothesize, what percent of your current employees are advocates of the company? Why or why not?

   a.

8. **In your opinion, do your current vendors and/or clients advocate on behalf of your company?**

   If you had to hypothesize, do current vendors and/or clients adore your brand enough to advocate on behalf of the company? Why or why not?

   a.

9. **In your opinion, do your current customers advocate on behalf of your company?**

   If you had to hypothesize, do current consumers adore your brand enough to advocate on behalf of the company? Why or why not?

   a.

PUTTING IT
ALL TOGETHER

COURAGE BRANDS WORK hard to have strong Central Courage Systems.

They tap into a Central Courage System to help them address business fears head-on by gathering knowledge, building faith, and then taking swift, intelligent action.

Courage Brands put in the time to know themselves completely, inside and out. They are unapologetic in what they stand for and are aware of what they will and won't compromise on. Courage Brands genuinely value their values. They know core values aren't eye rolls but, rather, how the exceptional roll. Courage Brands use those selected, prioritized values as their guides for decision making.

Courage Brands live their values and employ a Believership that abides by the company's core belief system. Courage Brands appoint a Believership that includes those who not only are Believers themselves but who are also worth believing in for other members of the organization. Leading the Believership is the person we call the Chief Belief Officer and who serves as the face of the company.

The sole goal of the Believership is to make Believers in all directions: your staff, your customers, your prospects, the media, and if a public company, your board and Wall Street.

The Believership, within the walls of the company, makes either Believers or Fake Believers. The way to make Believers is by having total alignment from the top down, by empowering teams to take ownership of their job, by genuinely caring about people, and by taking actions that mirror their words.

The Believership is also responsible for unearthing the company's toughest business fears. One way to do this is by delegating.

A Believership can form and assign an experimental task force (ETF) to a complicated, futuristic fear. This group, composed of a competent, diverse group of internal Believers, is given the time, space, and budget to recommend a course of action to the Believership on how to conquer the business fear.

Courage Brands are aware that fear and courage are brothers—they cannot get to courage without first having fear. Courage Brands understand that fear is ordinary and that everyone has fears. Hence, Courage Brands turn fears into friends. Instead of suppressing them, they address them. They realize their fears and turn them into tangible objects. A Courage Brand's ETF, ever so focused, often works together to shrink the largest fear in front of them before moving on to anything else.

A Believership may employ multiple ETFs on multiple fears at the same time. It may have an ETF conquering an industry blind spot while another is focused on shrinking a product, service, or perception fear.

Once a fear is brought to the surface, Courage Brands inject a sense of urgency into a sensible plan. They do so by landing on and committing to a purpose. Courage Brands know their purpose must be truthful, purposeful, emotional, and differential. They know they must insert a "rally cry inside their why," which helps them motivate and maintain their mission-focused talent, while also attracting new employees (aka future Believers) to the cause.

With a newly minted purpose, Courage Brands then begin to devise a plan on how to execute for tomorrow. They understand the importance of taking action and "playing offense" through the creation of courageous new offerings or messages.

When it comes to creating innovative new products or services, Courage Brands should look to become an industry fear in their category. Courage Brands swiftly put ETFs in place—comprised of competent, diverse players from multiple departments—to perform their cover-and-move strategy. Their elastic purposes allow Courage Brands to continue to "cover" their current products while working to "move" toward their next revenue stream or innovation.

When it's time to execute a new message, Courage Brands should narrowcast to influencers with an authentic, aspirational, and amazing story. In a media-obese world, Courage Brands can provoke meaningful participation by tapping into the four P's of advocacy—Point of View, Precision, Passion, and Promoters.

Putting it all together, Courage Brands stay relevant by using their Central Courage System to make fast, calculated decisions. Having an established Central Courage System in place makes it easier for them to pull the trigger in a blink on unified decisions. Courage Brands know that when it's go time, the team can maximize its *Return on Courage* by making smarter, swifter, and most important, effective decisions that propel the entire company—product, brand, staff, and all—clearly forward.

YOUR ULTIMATE RETURN ON COURAGE

"I show up in a pair of old boat shoes, no socks. A dirty pair of jeans, a black T-shirt, and a red ski jacket. I've flown down from Vancouver, from Whistler the night before. I haven't shaved. I didn't know I was going so that's how I interviewed for the job as head of global marketing for Apple."
—Steve Wilhite

YOU NEED TO be brave when you go into business with one of the world's shrewdest visionaries. Lucky for now-retired Steve Wilhite, he has always had courage and a keen sense of what matters most to him. It was one of the reasons he felt confident riding the Steve Jobs wave as Apple's vice president of global marketing.[1]

Wilhite recalls of his time with Jobs, "He was looking to surround himself with people that he respected, but people who were not afraid, who were not fearful of telling him what they thought and why they thought it. He would challenge people in really direct, aggressive ways, and if you weren't willing or able to defend your point of view, you're fired, you're done, I got no use for you."

Those two years at Apple were part of an illustrious, high-stakes career in which Wilhite also held multiple leadership roles at major automotive companies like Nissan, Volkswagen of America, and Hyundai. In 1998 Wilhite led the VW team that was recognized by *Ad Age* as Marketer of the Year. A few years later, he steered Nissan's global brand, which came with a $3 billion annual budget. In 2007, as the chief operating officer of Hyundai, Wilhite helped the company break records in unit volume and revenue performance while also rebuilding trust with the Hyundai Dealer Council.[2]

With big jobs come big budgets and often even bigger egos, but this never deterred Wilhite from staying true to himself. "I never worried about being fired from a job," he says. "I never worried about public opinion. I never worried about criticism. I always understood that criticism is a data point. It's one person's perspective at one moment in time."[3]

Wilhite is an embodiment of "me complete me," with his exceptional sense of self-awareness, which made it easy for him to know precisely what he wanted in a career. It can be distilled down to one word: challenges.

But many of us don't embrace issues as easily as Wilhite. It can be a struggle to put our teams in a position to be able to face their challenges. Also, when taking on complicated business problems, internal hurdles don't help. They slow us down and can prevent us from conquering the loftiest of challenges.

Internal strife exists when there's a lack of alignment at the Believership level. This detours many employees off their path and can lead to inaction. "At the end of the day, businesses or churches, social organizations or athletic teams are a reflection of the values of the leaders," Wilhite says. "A leader's effectiveness is often measured by how well they inculcate their values in other team members and employees."

For all his years in business, the key to Wilhite's success was looking deep within himself, then asking the hard question: Was he genuinely buying what his Believership was selling?

"I needed to buy in," he says. "I needed to buy in to the products, the services, to what I believe are the underlying values of the company. That's not everybody. That's just me."

Wilhite readily admits he has worked in a number of environments where he didn't buy in. As a Fake Believer, he knew it was time to move on.

"Leaving companies is always hard," he says. "You're leaving some friends. You're leaving security. You're leaving your paycheck. You don't necessarily have something better to go to, but ultimately, if you acquiesce, and you just say I'm going to settle for this, you give up some of your soul."

Change, like fear, is constant. Again, fear and courage are brothers. We cannot pursue a courageous feat if we first don't overtly attack our business fear head-on.

Wilhite sets the right tone when he says, "If you ever want to be great, you have to risk failure. There's a risk-reward curve that exists. It's not a perfectly smooth curve but generally low risk, low return. There is something about courageous brands that don't want to settle for that low return."

Setting yourself up to maximize your Return on Courage is adhering to the five steps of P.R.I.C.E. to successfully establish your Central Courage System. To set up your Central Courage System is to set up your process for success.

Businesses cannot be courageous. Only the people inside a business hold the potential to create a Courage Brand. This type of action is a choice. When you *choose courage*, you willingly accept that the journey starts by unlocking your personal courage first.

Wilhite sums it up when he says, "Ultimately, courage is based on values and training. Do I have the values and belief system to make the courageous decision, to make the right decision, in spite of the cultural environment that I exist in and in spite of the differences that might exist between me and the client that I'm serving?"

There will be moments when instead of driving change, change will drive you. Hence, you must be prepared for this by having your Central Courage System in place before you need it. It takes discipline to train your team to follow this process, especially when it seems like nothing to date is currently wrong in your business. In fact, when things are good is the best time to act.

Remember, it's of utmost importance to be prepared. Have your Believership in place, and create a diverse experimental task force now to best deal with any hardships that may come your way tomorrow.

Today, having a superior product is not enough. Consumers have an ocean of endless choices at their disposal. What separates TOMS from other shoe brands or Apple from the 300 undifferentiated personal computing companies is that they have made themselves *meaningful.*

If you're in the business of business, you're expected to make something that's both useful and meaningful. To be meaningful is to mean more than your competitor in the mind of your audience. It means you have already achieved courageous feats that place you in the heart, minds, and mouths of advocates everywhere.

To be meaningful is to be courageous.

As a focusing device, I like to remind my clients that CMO, which stands for Chief Marketing Officer, should be replaced with Chief *Meaningful* Officer. Our primary job is to help chief marketing officers make the courageous choices to morph their businesses into willing Courage Brands. After all, Courage Brands are obsessed over by consumers while Coward Brands—which I explain in detail at my online venture Courage Bootcamp—are all but obsolete.

Courage Brands display valor in the face of hardship, then make the conscious decision to act on it. Courage Brands confront uncertainty boldly and are brave enough to do something about it. Courage Brands have a strong point of view about the consequences of letting threats run unchecked.

Courage Brands aren't waiting around to see if they'll become part of the Business Apocalypse. (Remember former Cisco CEO John Chambers' death prediction for companies that we discussed in Chapter 1?) Instead, they take action to relevantly propel themselves into tomorrow.

Most of all, Courage Brands don't just weather whatever circumstances may come their way gracefully. Courage Brands shrink fear and, ultimately, transform.

Courage Brands don't just survive.

Courage Brands rise, thrive, and win.

RETURN ON COURAGE HELPS COMPANIES MAXIMIZE THEIR RETURN ON INVESTMENT

Most businesses are properly focused on return on investment. Courage Brands have a high Return on Courage. How can you recognize when your brand is moving down the right path to delivering a Return on Courage?

HERE ARE FIVE KEY RETURN ON COURAGE MOMENTS:

1. COMMUNICATION: Lead with your company's values

By doing the hard work of setting up your Central Courage System, you're on your way to eliminating the fragmented gap that sits between organizational health and courageous business.

All decisions can now be made the right way—through your

core values. Remember, core values are not eye rolls. They are how the exceptional roll. Knowing your values and communicating them takes the guessing game out of what matters most to your business. Activated properly, your values become your corporate cadence that can bring calm and alignment to your employees.

Remember, repeating makes Believers. The same holds true when you stay authentic to your values and use them as decision-making filters.

2. CONVICTION: Make internal Believers

When you lead with your values, you have the opportunity to make a Believer. When you make internal Believers, you make a culture. When you have a culture crafted out of your values and belief system, you build a loyal company willing to go the distance on your behalf. This is the idea of conviction. How you operate and communicate is the driving force behind making Believers or making Fake Believers. It has never been more desired by a next generation workforce than it is now.

In less than a decade, 75 percent of your workforce will be Millennials. This generation aspires to work at unique, innovative, and purpose-driven companies. They'll stick around if they believe. Create an authentic, empowering, and purpose-driven work environment that Believers can rally behind.

3. CLARITY: Proactively know your business fears

If worrying about what could cause your business to fail is keeping you up at night, then it's time to audit your business fears. Know-how is the key to it all: the ability to smoke out and discover business fears that have previously stayed hidden. Gaining clarity in regards to these tumultuous hurdles is half the battle. Your team should be fully aware of the problems in your industry, your brand, and your product that you are relentlessly trying to combat. Remember, either you drive change or change could destroy you.

Once you have total awareness of these fears, you can begin to shrink them down, eliminate noise, and stay focused on the initiatives that matter most. This is clarity at work.

4. CAUSE: Ignite external advocates

When your message courageously stands for something meaningful, you unlock passionate external Believers who will advocate on your behalf—everywhere they go—so long as you stay true, purposeful, and consistent to the cause.

Great causes have a clear enemy. So find a big, juicy enemy to take down, such as greed, injustice, or repression. Remember, to inject a rally cry in your why and consider creating a call *for* action—which always tops a call *to* action—to move the cause forward.

You now know how to create an authentic, aspirational, and amazing message. You now understand how to share this message through narrowcasting and promoters. When you do, thanks to passionate external Believers, unlimited earned media opportunities are possible.

5. CHANGE: Your business evolves—it avoids stasis or, worse, death

Is your primary business goal to sustain relevance? Is it to change and transform your business as you grow? Both goals set out to increase the preference for your business by adding meaningful new messages or modern core competencies to the organization. By doing either, you have done what less than half of Fortune 500 businesses have been able to do in the past 15 years—survive.

Becoming a Courage Brand does not guarantee success. But remaining stagnant and working solely for incremental gains are not strategies for surviving the rough, patchy, unpredictable business waters of the next decade.

That's the thing about courageous companies. Establishing your Central Courage System is simply courageous preparation. When you follow the steps of P.R.I.C.E., when you play offense and drive change, you put yourself in a good position to evolve, thrive, and win.

When courageous business decisions are successfully made, it's like traffic opening up on a five-lane highway. This allows companies to stay proactive, not just be protective.

The key word here is *success*. With triumph—small and big—the floodgates of possibility start to present themselves, and your staff will thrive off that opportunistic energy.

When courage works at the workplace, it becomes easier to choose courage in the office again and again. It contagiously spreads all across your team, office, and culture.

Courage, in fact, breeds courage.

With it, corporate confidence grows and morale balloons.

Conversely, with failure, for many, fear breeds fear. When this happens, you can feel a negative dissenting poison permeating through the company's culture.

Activating courage in a healthy workplace is like learning how to ride a bike. At first, it may feel daunting. You know there will be lots of scrapes and bruises. But once your balance stabilizes and you get those wheels moving, momentum ensues, and it's hard to go back to anything else.

EPILOGUE

Don't just look at the world differently.
Do the world differently.
—Ryan Berman

As the chief marketing officer joins me on the phone, I can already tell this will be an unfortunate waste of time for both of us. It's just after I remind him that most of my questions will be about business courage—or the lack of it—that he breaks the disappointing news.

Counsel from his internal public relations team has shut down the idea of this interview being used in the book. The conversation is pleasant as he offers up one of his C-suite cohorts from another business that would make a good sound bite or conversation instead.

He then wishes me well. I do the same to him, and we both hang up.

Throughout the book-writing process, I encountered a handful of phone calls like this one. In almost every scenario, the brands that most Americans would consider not courageous go down just like this. Fear of what I may write rules their roost, and because of that, they pass.

Then there was an entirely different group of willing business professionals. These individuals openly shared their stories. They were truthful on the glorious positives and gloomy pitfalls of their business.

There is a compelling insight here.

Willing Ascenders were open to being interviewed. These people embraced the realities of their yesterday and today and their desire to innovate tomorrow.

Cautionary Descenders were the ones who denied interview access. They said a lot by choosing not to say anything.

Willing Ascenders courageously played offense to evolve their business forward. Cautionary Descenders were almost always stuck, protecting share, forced into playing defense.

Though I never got the chance to ask, I've surmised that for most Cautionary Descenders it's not that they don't believe courage has a role in their organizations, it's that they don't believe they can convince senior management to consider making the necessary but often brutally hard changes.

Throughout this journey, I've tried to help you arrive at a more courageous destination. After devoting more than 1,000 days to the topic—interviewing the brave and the brilliant, sponging up topical books by authors who inspire me—what I know for certain is that you'll never achieve "high risk, high reward" without first realizing that high risk demands high courage.

More so, employing courage decreases the chance for personal regret.

I believe it's not enough to simply look at the world differently. You have to courageously take action to *do the world differently.* When it comes to doing, persistently do so with knowledge, faith, and intelligent action. Learning courage is not the end. It's a means to an end. And that end, that outcome, is doing something meaningful.

The profound words of Lao-tzu wisely remind us, "When I let go of what I am, I become what I might be."[1]

Last I checked, the robots have yet to take over. Which means this is a book about the power of potential in people. I now know my life goal is not to live as long as I can; it's to live as fully as I can. The creation of this manuscript catapulted me onto my purposeful quest to help others infectiously act with courage.

If I can help a few folks have the courage to pass this book along to their bosses, if I can flip a handful of Cautionary Descenders into Willing Ascenders by igniting a difficult, courageous conversation within the walls of their organizations, then my journey was worth it.

Courage is the catalyst for an evolving you. It can help you liberate yourself from the competition and from Fake Believers. Most of all, it can help you liberate yourself from *yourself.*

It can shift you from a transactional business into a transformational one. It can boost you forward not just in your business life but also in your personal life. It can help you maximize your human potential and make the most of your short time on this planet.

My hope is that you can benefit from learning how to implement courage into your routine decision-making process and that you will revert back to *Return on Courage* when you need some useful inspiration that can transform yourself, your team, or your business as you move forward. If you've made it this far, and the book leaves you wanting more, you can also turn to Courage Bootcamp, my eight-week online course that helps you operationalize courage throughout your company. What I've learned from my own book-writing journey is that not only are we afraid of change but also that change itself is hard! Courage Bootcamp helps you install courage in your organization by first instilling courage in your people. If you aspire to unlock your competitive advantage, we can train you to do so at Courage Bootcamp.

What *will* you do with your finite time here? When all is said and done, will you make the world better or simply *your* world better?

If you get it right, it can be both.

SEVEN UNWAVERING TRAITS OF COURAGE BRANDS

1. **Courage Brands are unapologetic in who they are.** They aren't trying to be all things to all people. Their core values are known, valued, prioritized, and lived. Knowing their truth makes it easier for Courage Brands to attract passionate core believers.

2. **Courage Brands put a "rally cry in their why."** They know a call *for* action always tops a call *to* action. Finding their rally cry helps them create their company's cause where Believers want to stick around and help create momentum that leads to a movement.

3. **Courage Brands inject a sense of urgency into a sensible plan.** They articulate "why this story now" and they do so by understanding the pressing contextual relevance of what is happening now. It all gets thoughtfully rolled out as a comprehensive program.

4. **Courage Brands lead with the brand's creature versus the product features.** They don't get bogged down leading with product features. They lead with their unapologetic, purposeful point of view.

5. **Courage Brands create passionate Believers.** Courage Brands and their Believership always put Believers first. It's why Courage Brands have passionate employees, products, services, and messages that attract true external Believers.

6. **Courage Brands narrowcast to advocates who broadcast to the rest of the world.** Courage Brands narrowcast to influential promoters who proudly spread the gospel of Courage Brands' messages through word of mouth, social media, and other social networks. Courage Brands are prepared to give full control of their brands to these Believers—greenlighting those advocates to broadcast those meaningful messages to the masses.

7. **Courage Brands address business fears head-on.** They continue to address (versus suppress) business fears and industry blind spots. The Believership may call upon an internal experimental task force and give them time, space, and money to recommend a solution to shrink a fear or blind spot.

YOUR CENTRAL COURAGE SYSTEM COMES WITH A P.R.I.C.E.

ORGANIZATIONAL HEALTH ORGANIZATIONAL HEALTH ORGANIZATIONAL HEALTH	COURAGEOUS BUSINESS COURAGEOUS BUSINESS COURAGEOUS BUSINESS COURAGEOUS BUSINESS

P R I C E

PRIORITIZE THROUGH VALUES	RALLY BELIEVERS	IDENTIFY FEARS	COMMIT TO A PURPOSE	EXECUTE YOUR ACTION

VALUES ARROW ⟶
_____

VALUE YOUR VALUES
_____

KNOW YOUR VALUES
Me Complete Me

PRIORITIZE VALUES
_____

LIVE YOUR VALUES
_____

BELIEVERSHIP VS LEADERSHIP
CBO Chief Believe Officer
_____

MAKE BELIEVERS OR FAKE BELIEVERS
Respecting Makes Believers
Repeating Makes Believers
Caring Makes Believers
Seeing Is Believing
_____

EXPERIMENTAL TASK FORCE (ETF)
Reports Into Believership
_____

INDUSTRY FEARS
Industry Blind Spots

PRODUCT FEARS

SERVICE FEARS

PERCEPTION FEARS
_____

PERSONAL FEARS
Our Central Nervous Systems Don't Help
_____

MUST BE TRUTHFUL
The Truth Helps
_____

MUST BE PURPOSEFUL
Put "Rally Cry In Your Why"
_____

MUST BE EMOTIONAL
Call For Action
Vs. Call To Action
_____

MUST BE DIFFERENTIAL
Different Is The Difference
_____

PURPOSE ELASTICITY
Wide Enough Purpose To Create New Rev Streams
_____

NEW OFFERING
Etf: Create The Industry Fear
Master Zaggers: Cover & Move
_____

NEW MESSAGING
FourP's Of Advocacy

POV
Market "Creature" Vs. Features

PASSION
Rational Tells, Irrational Sells

PRECISION
Do Leadership > Thought Leadership

PROMOTERS
Narrowcast to Influencers
_____

PRIORITIZE THROUGH VALUES

Core values are not eye rolls. They are how
the exceptional roll.

How do you know when to take a stance if you don't know what you
stand for? Core values are the modern-day rudders of decision making. Many businesses are missing the mark as to what the next generation truly values. Most must realize that the next generation won't buy
unless they *buy in*. With thousands of choices at their fingertips, the
differentiator is valuing, declaring, and living your distinct core values.

RALLY BELIEVERS

The goal of leadership is Believership. Make
Believers versus Fake Believers.

Companies that genuinely emote their values attract mission-cen-
tric internal Believers who live those values. These Believers aren't
just wanted—they are needed. The sole goal of your Believership is
to make Believers in all directions—with your staff, your customers,
and your board. One critical step of rallying Believers is moving on
from Fake Believers.

IDENTIFY YOUR FEARS

> Fear and courage are brothers. Address (versus suppress) business fears directly.

Once internal Believers are in place, companies can begin to attack their largest business fears. There are four business fears to regularly audit and assess: (1) industry fears, (2) product fears, (3) service fears, and (4) perception fears. Once you are through the largest fear, address the next largest with internal Believers—or an assigned experimental task force (ETF). Grant ETFs sufficient time, space, and budget to provide recommendations or smoke out future fears or industry blind spots.

COMMIT TO YOUR PURPOSE

> Inject a "rally cry in your why." A call *for* action tops a call *to* action.

When it comes to choosing a worthy company purpose, look to inject a "rally cry within your why" so internal Believers stick around and external Believers join your cause. This rallying cry must be truthful, purposeful, emotional, and differential. Many worthy purposes shine light on an enemy and work hard to bring that chosen evil down. It's critical that brands choose a wide enough purpose that allows them to stretch their offerings as they evolve into the future. We call this *Purpose Elasticity.*

EXECUTE YOUR ACTION

New Offering? Cover and Move.
New Messaging? The Four P's of advocacy.

New Offering: Companies use their elastic purpose to blaze new proactive offerings that keep them speeding forward. Cover your current products or services while you're working on moving toward your next revenue stream or innovation. Activate your ETF to evolve or transform your company, and courageously set out to become the industry fear.

New Messaging: There are more ways than ever for people to block you. Noise is at an all-time high while consumer attention spans are at a staggering all-time low. In a media-obese, ad-blocking world where many prefer to hear from friends, coworkers, and loved ones, executing for advocacy is the critical difference. The four P's of advocacy successfully help your meaningful message break through:

Point of View: Market your singular unapologetic brand creature, not your plethora of product features.

Precision: Execute with excellence. Thought leadership is nothing without do leadership.

Passion: Rational tells; irrational sells—a "rational tell" only justifies a passionate purchase.

Promoters: Plant your ideas and narrowcast to believing influencers who, in turn, broadcast to the rest on your behalf.

CORE VALUES ASSESSMENT

Remember:

1. Core values are not eye rolls. They are how the exceptional roll!
2. Once you know what you stand for, you know when to take a stand.

Follow the below steps and truly strip away anything but the core of what matters most to you. When you have completed this exercise, you will know where to spend your time and, better yet, where not to put your energy. This includes people as much as projects.

- Viscerally jot down the 8–10 words that pop out.
- Step away from your choices for 24–48 hours.
- Cut it to 5–6 words.
- Write a paragraph as to why you chose each value for you.
- Choose values that drive behavior. Avoid "Just In Case" values.
- Be critical. Keep solely the essential values. If you can, cut it to 3–5.
- Prioritize the values from most important to 4th (or 3rd/5th).
- Share with partners or Believership.
- Lock in values, or, work with partners to merge partner values into 3–4 Guiding Principles the company can live by.

Core Values List

Accomplishment	Creativity	Good will
Abundance	Credibility	Goodness
Accountability	Decisiveness	Gratitude
Accuracy	Democracy	Hard work
Achievement	Determination	Harmony
Adventure	Discipline	Healing
Approval	Discovery	Holistic Living
Autonomy	Diversity	Honesty
Balance	Education	Honor
Beauty	Efficiency	Improvement
Challenge	Environment	Independence
Change	Equality	Individuality
Clarity	Excellence	Initiative
Cleanliness, orderliness	Exploration	Inner peace
Collaboration	Fairness	Innovation
Commitment	Faith	Integrity
Communication	Faithfulness	Intelligence
Community	Family	Intensity
Compassion	Flair	Intimacy
Competence	Flexibility	Intuition
Competition	Forgiveness	Joy
Concern for others	Freedom	Justice
Confidence	Friendship	Knowledge
Connection	Frugality	Leadership
Conservation	Fulfillment	Learning
Content over form	Fun	Love
Cooperation	Generosity	Loyalty
Coordination	Genuineness	Meaning

Merit	Quality over quantity	Service
Moderation	Quantity over quality	Simplicity
Modesty	Reciprocity	Sincerity
Money	Recognition	Skill
Nature	Regularity	Solitude
Nurturing	Relaxation	Speed
Obedience	Reliability	Spirituality
Open-mindedness	Resourcefulness	Stability
Openness	Respect for others	Standardization
Optimism	Responsibility	Status
Patriotism	Responsiveness	Straightforwardness
Peace, Nonviolence	Results	Strength
Perfection	Romance	Success
Perseverance	Rule of law	Systemization
Persistence	Sacrifice	Teamwork
Personal growth	Safety	Thoughtfulness
Personal health	Satisfying others	Timeliness
Playfulness	Security	Tolerance
Pleasure	Self-awareness	Tradition
Power	Self-confidence	Tranquility
Practicality	Self-esteem	Trust
Preservation	Self-expression	Trustworthiness
Privacy	Self-improvement	Truth
Problem solving	Self-love	Unity
Professionalism	Self-mastery	Variety
Progress	Self-reliance	Vitality
Prosperity	Self-trust	Wealth
Purpose	Sensuality	Wisdom

ACKNOWLEDGMENTS

THIS HERCULEAN EFFORT was a *we* thing, not a *me* thing.

I want to thank the following four types of luminaries I leaned on for the creation of *Return on Courage:*

Filed under *brave mavericks* are many of the folks you first think of when you picture courage. This included Navy SEAL Jeff Boss, astronaut Loretta Hidalgo, Army infantryman Nick Paea, tornado chaser Reed Timmer, retired fireman Mike Rubino, ER physician Joe Bellezzo, bank teller robbed at gunpoint Patricia Chapin-Bayley, *MasterChef* winner Claudia Sandoval, CBS anchor Carlo Cecchetto, and flight attendant Steven Slater.

Under *brain masters*, I want to thank University of Colorado Hospital oncology system director Thomas Purcell, Cambridge University immunology PhD Nicholas Alp, NeuroGym CEO John Assaraf, and clinical psychologists Emily Cox-Martin, Tanisha Joshi, and Elissa Kolva.

Under *bullish business maestros*, I was fortunate to interview founders, cofounders, CEOs, presidents, chief marketing officers, and many others from Amazon, AND 1, Apple, B Lab, Domino's, Fender, Google, Hostess, Live Nation, Method, Qualcomm, Stone Brewery, Tuft & Needle, Uber, Zappos, and many more. Special shout-outs to Brian Enge, Jay Coen Gilbert, Tony Hsieh, Evan Jones, Greg Koch, Roger Martin, Daehee Park, Jeff Ragovin, Burke Raine, Manny Rodriguez,

Eric Ryan, Jason Spero, Andrew Turner, Russell Wallach, Russell Weiner, Steve Wilhite, and Tyler Williams.

Finally, under *inspiring authors,* I was truly influenced by the ideas of Grant Cardone, Jim Collins, Seth Godin, Adam Grant, Verne Harnish, Sally Hogshead, James Kerr, Bryan Kramer, Patrick Lencioni, Steve McKee, Greg McKeown, and Elise Mitchell.

A thousand kisses to my wife, Randy, for believing in me and for allowing me to leave her at home on a regular basis with our sweet, imaginative six-year-old son and our amazingly sunny three-year-old daughter. My motivations for writing this book have indeed changed throughout this journey. In total candor, at first I was scribing the world's heaviest business card. Now, it's clear this book is first for my kids. As always, I love you both with all my heart, all my mind, and all my soul.

I'd like to thank my two previous business partners, Jon Bailey and Indra Bowers. You gave me the time and a budget to tackle this important topic. Without that, there was no way this book got completed.

I have made so many new friends from going on this journey. To those brilliant, ambitious souls who gave me their scarce resource of time for interviews, I genuinely hope I did you justice.

To all my coworkers who assisted in bringing *Return on Courage* to life, thank you! Specific shout-outs to Billy Collins, Deena Betcher, and Beth Wilkinson for being on my hip and truly believing in the concept. Thank you to Daniel Andreani, Amy Antony, Amanda Duncan, Mike Fennessy, Amy Gelender, Justin Hiew, Austin Lane, Aki Martin, Julie Messing, Joe Nafziger, Scojo, Nathan Smith, and James White. No one reaches their goals alone, and I thank you for your counsel, commentary, and constructive criticisms.

Perhaps unbeknownst to John Assaraf, James Bachman, Ron Berger, Jason Deland, Dean McBeth, Darrell Pilant, Joan Waltman, Steve Wilhite, and Jerry Yen, you all inspired me to pour all I could into this project. Not only is the book exponentially improved, but I am also exponentially improved because of all of you. Thank you for making me better.

To my go-to research mavericks, Jill Avery, Sterling Doak, Bo Frazier, Liz Gasser, Gayle Malone, Tommy Miers, Drew Weber, and Amy Winhoven—you all contributed to the ideas found in these pages.

To my Old Bay–loving surface editor Ron Donoho—thank you for your positive attitude and help. I'm so glad you were inspired by this project. And to fellow writer Emily Belden, for helping me navigate this new book space territory. You made the book so much better! San Diego will miss you.

To the full team at Greenleaf, thank you for making me sound like a credible author. Lindsey Clark, specifically, I like your style. Thanks for taking it easy on me, Judy Marchman!

To Julie Broad and the Book Launchers squad, thanks for having my back on bringing *Return on Courage* to life.

Finally, to my parents, my brother Matt, my cousin Jamie, and to all the Bermans and Chvotkins: Who could have ever imagined we'd go from *Bo Knows Bo* to this? I learned that no matter how much distance is between us, a family that laughs together stays together.

This book is only this book because of all of you.

NOTES

INTRODUCTION

1. Grant Cardone, *The 10X Rule* (Hoboken, New Jersey: John Wiley & Sons, 2011).

PART 1: A TASTE OF COURAGE

1. Russell Weiner, phone interview with Ryan Berman, June 1, 2016.
2. Neal Freyman, "Doyle Rules: After a Job Well Done, the CEO of Domino's Prepares to Leave," *Morning Brew*, January 21, 2018, https://www.morningbrew.com/stories/doyle-rules-after-a-job-well-done-the-ceo-of-dominos-prepares-to-leave/.
3. Weiner, interview.
4. Statista, Yahoo Finance, *Business Insider*, Tech Chart of the Day, Present Value as of March 23, 2017.
5. Weiner, interview.
6. Steve McKee, *When Growth Stalls: How It Happens, Why You're Stuck & What to Do About It* (San Francisco: Jossey-Bass, 2009).

CHAPTER 1: THE BUSINESS APOCALYPSE

1. Thomas Purcell, in-person interview with Ryan Berman, May 31, 2016.
2. DXC Sponsored Content in *Harvard Business Review*, "Digital Transformation Is Racing Ahead and No Industry Is Immune," HBR.org, July 19, 2017, https://hbr.org/sponsored/2017/07/digital-transformation-is-racing-ahead-and-no-industry-is-immune-2.
3. Kim Gittleson, "Can a Company Live Forever?," BBC News, January 19, 2012, https://www.bbc.com/news/business-16611040.

4. Mark J. Perry/AEIdeas, "Fortune 500 Firms in 1955 vs 2014; 88% Are Gone, and We're All Better Off Because of that Dynamic 'Creative Destruction,'" AEI.org, August 18, 2014, http://www.aei.org/publication/fortune-500-firms-in-1955-vs-2014-89-are-gone-and-were-all-better-off-because-of-that-dynamic-creative-destruction/.

5. Martin Reeves and Lisanne Pueschel, "Die Another Day: What Leaders Can Do About the Shrinking Life Expectancy of Corporations," October 2016, http://img-stg.bcg.com/ BCG-Die-Another-Day-Dec-2015_tcm9-76807.pdf.

6. Bill Carmondy, "Why 96% of Businesses Fail Within 10 Years," *Inc.*, August 12, 2015, https://www.inc.com/bill-carmody/why-96-of-businesses-fail-within-10-years.html.

7. Eric Wagner, "Five Reasons 8 Out of 10 Businesses Fail," *Forbes*, September 2013, https://www.forbes.com/sites/ericwagner/2013/09/12/ five-reasons-8-out-of-10-businesses-fail/#49064c836978.

8. McKee, *When Growth Stalls*.

9. Ewing Marion Kauffman Foundation, "Entrepreneurship Is on the Rise but Long-Term Startup Decline Leaves Millions of Americans Behind," February 16, 2017, https://www. kauffman.org/newsroom/2017/2/entrepreneurship-is-on-the-rise-but-long-term-startup-decline-leaves-millions-of-americans-behind.

10. Jim Collins and Morten Hansen, *Great by Choice* (New York: Harper Collins, 2011).

11. Julie Bort, "Retiring Cisco CEO Delivers Dire Prediction: 40% of Companies Will Be Dead in 10 years," *Business Insider*, June 8, 2015, http://www.businessinsider.com/ chambers-40-of-companies-are-dying-2015-6.

12. Bernard Marr, "Big Data: 20 Mind-Boggling Facts Everyone Must Read," *Forbes*, September 30, 2015, https://www.forbes.com/sites/bernardmarr/2015/09/30/ big-data-20-mind-boggling-facts-everyone-must-read/#12d7da7917b1.

13. Timothy Aeppel, "50 Million Users: The Making of an 'Angry Birds' Internet Meme," WSJ Blog, March 20, 2015, https://blogs.wsj.com/ economics/2015/03/20/50-million-users-the-making-of-an-angry-birds-internet-meme/.

14. Traci Lengel, and Mike Kuczala, *The Kinesthetic Classroom: Teaching and Learning Through Movement* (Thousand Oaks, CA: Corwin, 2010); Kevin McSpadden, "You Now Have a Shorter Attention Span Than a Goldfish," *Time*, May 14, 2015, http://time. com/3858309/attention-spans-goldfish/.

15. "Most Millennials Have Installed Ad Blockers," eMarketer, October 13, 2016, https:// www.emarketer.com/Article/Most-Millennials-Have-Installed-Ad-Blockers/1014592.

16. "30% of all Internet Users Will Ad Block by 2018," *Business Insider*, March 23, 2017, http://www.businessinsider.com/30-of-all-internet-users-will-ad-block-by-2018-2017-3.

17. Jason Lynch, "New Study Says by 2025, Half of Consumers Under 32 Won't Pay for Cable," *AdWeek*, October 6, 2015, https://www.adweek.com/tv-video/ new-study-says-2025-half-consumers-under-32-won-t-pay-cable-167400/.

18. Louis V. Gerstner Jr., *Who Says Elephants Can't Dance?* (New York: Harper Collins, 2002).

19. Manny Rodriguez, in-person interview with Ryan Berman, May 31, 2016.

20. Tony Hsieh, email exchange with Ryan Berman, July 17, 2018.

21. "News Release: Three Years Later, U.S. Companies Continue to Struggle With Innovation, Accenture Survey Reveals," Accenture, March 21, 2016, https://newsroom.accenture.com/news/three-years-later-us-companies-continue-to-struggle-with-innovation-accenture-survey-reveals.htm.

22. Brian Enge, phone interview with Ryan Berman, July 2018.

23. Jason Spero, phone interview with Ryan Berman, June 2016.

24. Jay Coen Gilbert, phone interview with Ryan Berman, July 2016.

25. Nicholas Alp, phone interview with Ryan Berman, June 2016.

26. Roger Martin, in-person interview with Ryan Berman, June 2016.

27. Deloitte Millennial Survey 2018, https://www2.deloitte.com/global/en/pages/about-deloitte/articles/millennialsurvey.html#.

28. John Ellett, "CMO Turnover Rate Reaches New High," *Forbes*, August 2, 2016, accessed on RussellReynolds.com, http://www.russellreynolds.com/newsroom/cmo-turnover-reaches-new-high.

29. Jonathan Mildenhall, "Fearless Marketing Drives AirBnB," WARC, December 2, 2015, https://www.warc.com/newsandopinion/news/fearless_marketing_drives_airbnb/35826.

30. Kevin Daum, "22 Quotes from Salvador Dali That Creatively Inspire Success," *Inc.*, https://www.inc.com/kevin-daum/22-quotes-from-salvador-dali-that-creatively-inspire-success.html.

CHAPTER 2: THE SIX COURAGE MYTHS

1. *New Oxford American Dictionary,* Apple computer edition, accessed August 23, 2015.

2. Coleman Herbert, phone interview with Ryan Berman, June 2016.

3. Jill Avery, in-person interview with Ryan Berman at Harvard Business School, June 2016.

4. Weiner, interview.

5. Andrew Turner, Skype interview with Ryan Berman, May 31, 2016.

6. Weiner, interview.

7. Justin Sablich, "Trip Advisor to Stop Selling Tickets to Many Animal Attractions," *New York Times,* October 11, 2016, https://www.nytimes.com/2016/10/11/travel/tripadvisor-to-stop-selling-tickets-to-many-animal-attractions.html.

8. Adam Grant, *Originals: How Non-Conformists Move the World* (New York: Penguin, 2016).

9. Malcolm Gladwell, *Outliers: The Story of Success* (New York: Little, Brown & Company, 2008).

10. Kathleen Reardon, "Courage as a Skill," *Harvard Business Review,* January 2007, https://hbr.org/2007/01/courage-as-a-skill.

11. Bill Treasurer, "Courage Is the Key to Great Leadership," Entrepreneurs' Organization, https://www.eonetwork.org/octane-magazine/special-features/courageisthekeytogreatleadership.

12. Jeff Boss, phone interview with Ryan Berman, May 25, 2016.

13. Reardon, "Courage as a Skill."

14. Gilbert, interview.

15. Boss, interview.

16. Mike Rubino, email exchange with Ryan Berman, July 2016.

CHAPTER 3: COURAGEOUSLY REDEFINING COURAGE

1. Brené Brown, *Rising Strong: The Reckoning. The Rumble. The Revolution* (New York: Spiegel & Grau, 2015).

2. Cardone, *The 10X Rule.*

3. Dana Papke, "How this Amazing Maya Angelou Quote Applies to HR," TPO, May 27, 2015, http://www.tpo-inc.com/hr-audit-assessment/how-this-amazing-maya-angelou-quote-applies-to-hr-do-the-best-you-can-until-you-know-better-then-when-you-know-better-do-better/.

4. Richard Branson, *Business Stripped Bare: Adventures of a Global Entrepreneur* (New York: Penguin, 2008).

5. Mike Pearson, Facebook messenger exchange with Ryan Berman, July 2016.

6. Erin Littrell, email exchange with Ryan Berman, September 2016.

7. Grant, *Originals.*

8. Greg Kline, phone interview with Ryan Berman, September 2016.

9. Martin, interview.

10. Spero, interview.

11. Avery, interview.

12. Jocko Willink and Leif Babin, *Extreme Ownership: How Navy SEALs Lead and Win* (New York: St. Martin's Press, 2015).

13. Daehee Park, in-person interview with Ryan Berman, June 1, 2016.

14. Arthur Schopenhauer, *The World as Will and Idea*, Volume 1, preface to the first edition (1818), translated from the German by Richard Burdon Haldane and John Kemp in *The English and Foreign Philosophical Library: Volume XXII*, third edition (Boston, MA: Ticknor and Company, 1888), xv.

15. Park, interview.

16. Al Ries and Jack Trout, *Positioning: The Battle for Your Mind* (New York: McGraw-Hill, 2001).

17. Claudia Sandoval, in-person interview and email exchange with Ryan Berman, May 2016.

18. "After All Is Said and Done, More Is Said Than Done," The Daily Wit, July 15, 2008, https://supercynic.wordpress.com/2008/07/15/aesop/.

19. David Joseph Leingang, Exploring Leadership Solutions blog, http://daveleingang. com/home/in-any-moment-of-decision-the-best-thing-you-can-do-is-the-right-thing-the-next-best-thing-is-the-wrong-thing-and-the-worst-thing-you-can-do-is-nothing-theodore-roosevelt/.

20. Burke Raine, phone interview and email exchange with Ryan Berman, May 2016.

21. Japanese proverb in James Kerr, *Legacy: What the All Blacks Can Teach Us About the Business of Life* (London: Constable & Robinson, 2013).

22. Evan Jones, phone interview with Ryan Berman, May 23, 2016.

CHAPTER 4: THE FOUR PRINCIPLES OF COURAGE

1.   Ayetkin Tank, "I Owe My Great Talent Pool to a Tip from Steve Jobs," CNBC, September 27, 2016, https://www.cnbc.com/2016/09/27/steve-jobs-advice-on-hiring-helps-grow-this-ceos-talent-pool.html.

2.   Aimee Groth, "You're the Average of the Five People You Spend the Most Time With," *Business Insider*, July 24, 2012, http://www.businessinsider.com/jim-rohn-youre-the-average-of-the-five-people-you-spend-the-most-time-with-2012-7.

3.   Patty McCord, "How Netflix Reinvented HR," *Harvard Business Review*, January/February 2014, https://hbr.org/2014/01/how-netflix-reinvented-hr.

4.   Rudi Dalman, "Five Inspiring Quotes for HR Professionals," PeopleHR, October 20, 2016, https://www.peoplehr.com/blog/index.php/2016/10/20/five-inspiring-quotes-for-hr-professionals/.

5.   http://startupquotes.startupvitamins.com/post/141132813811/good-ideas-are-always-crazy-until-theyre-not.

6.   Thich Nhat Hanh, *Fear: Essential Wisdom for Getting Through the Storm* (New York: HarperCollins, 2012).

7.   Boss, interview.

8.   Jeff Ragovin, phone interview with Ryan Berman, May 25, 2016.

9.   Gilbert, interview.

10. Ekaterina Walter, "5 Myths of Leadership," *Forbes*, October 8, 2013, https://www.forbes.com/sites/ekaterinawalter/2013/10/08/5-myths-of-leadership/#266f5afc314e.

11. Russell Wallach, phone interview with Ryan Berman, June 2, 2016.

12. Sheryl Sandberg, 2016 Commencement Speech at University of California, Berkeley, http://news.berkeley.edu/2016/05/16/sheryl-sandberg-2016-commencement-address/.

13. Greg Koch, in-person interview at Stone Brewing with Ryan Berman, August 17, 2016.

14. Gerstner, *Who Says Elephants Can't Dance?*

15. Team YS, "The Story of Colonel Sanders," YourStory.com, July 2012, https://yourstory.com/2012/07/the-story-of-colonel-sanders-a-man-who-started-at-65-and-failed-1009-times-before-succeeding/.

16. Ashlee Vance, *Elon Musk: Tesla, SpaceX, and the Quest for a Fantastic Future* (New York: HarperCollins, 2015).

17. Vance, *Elon Musk.*

18. Boss, interview.

19. Carlo Cecchetto, email interview with Ryan Berman, February 2017.

20. Patricia Chapin-Bayley, Facetime interview with Ryan Berman, May 31, 2016.

21. Verne Harnish, *Scaling Up: How a Few Companies Make It . . . and Why the Rest Don't* (Ashburn, VA: Gazelles Inc., 2014).

22. Bobby Knight and Bob Hammel, *Knight: My Story* (New York: Thomas Dunne Books, 2002).

23. Alp, interview; John Assaraf, in-person interview with Ryan Berman, June 14, 2016.

24. Emily Cox-Martin, in-person interview with Ryan Berman, May 31, 2016.

25. Assaraf, interview.

PART 2: THE CENTRAL COURAGE SYSTEM

1. Seth Godin, *All Marketers Tell Stories* (New York: Penguin Group, 2009).

2. Collins and Hansen, *Great by Choice.*

3. Purcell, interview.

CHAPTER 5: PRIORITIZE THROUGH VALUES

1. Susan David and Christina Congleton, "Emotional Agility," *Harvard Business Review*, November 2013, https://hbr.org/2013/11/emotional-agility.

2. Afdhel Aziz, *Good Is the New Cool: Market Like You Give a Damn* (New York: Regan Arts, 2016).

3. Suzanne Vranica, "Average Tenure of CMO Continues to Decline," *Wall Street Journal*, March 17, 2017.

4. Kyle Russell, Apple Stakeholder Meeting, *Business Insider*, 2014, http://www.businessinsider.com/tim-cook-versus-a-conservative-think-tank-2014-2.

5. Park, interview.

6. James Fannin, "People and Purpose: What Amazon's Jeff Bezos Teaches Us About Values," IMS, July 1, 2014, http://www.ims.gs/blog/people-purpose-amazons-jeff-bezos-teaches-us-values/.

7. Tyler Williams, in-person interview with Ryan Berman, January 2016.

8. Darrell Pilant, email interview with Ryan Berman, January 2016.

9. Spero, interview.

10. Michelle Miller, "Flight Attendant Flips Out, Exits Via Chute," CBSNews.com, August 10, 2017, https://www.cbsnews.com/news/flight-attendant-flips-out-exits-via-chute/; James Barron, "JetBlue Flight Attendant Accepts Plea Deal," *New York Times* blog, City Room, October 19, 2010, https://cityroom.blogs.nytimes.com/2010/10/19/jetblue-flight-attendant-accepts-plea-deal/.

11. Steven Slater, phone interview with Ryan Berman, June 1, 2016.

12. Ted Reed, "JetBlue CEO: Slater's Act 'Egregious,'" *TheStreet*, August 30, 2010, https://www.thestreet.com/story/10847093/1/jetblue-ceo-slaters-act-egregious.html.

CHAPTER 6: RALLY BELIEVERS

1. Willink and Babin, *Extreme Ownership*.

2. "Effective Change Leadership Strategies," Four Corners Group, 2016, https://fourcornersgroup.com/from-the-corner-office-blog/effective-change-leadership-strategies/.

3. Park, interview.

4. Patrick Lencioni, *The Five Dysfunctions of a Team: A Leadership Fable* (San Francisco: Jossey-Bass, 2002).

5. Jones, interview.

6. Eric Ryan, Method, in-person interview with Ryan Berman, October 2, 2015.

7. Park, interview.

8. Wikipedia, s.v. "Pete Carroll," last edited 23 July 2018, 04:53, https://en.wikipedia.org/wiki/Pete_Carroll.

9. The Deloitte Millennial Study, "Big Demands and High Expectations," Deloitte, January 2014, https://www2.deloitte.com/content/dam/Deloitte/global/Documents/About-Deloitte/gx-dttl-2014-millennial-survey-report.pdf.

10. Katz Kiely, "The Talent War," CMO.com, February 12, 2016, https://www.cmo.com/features/articles/2016/2/11/the-talent-war.html#gs.APpluY0.

11. Ragovin, interview.

12. Harnish, *Scaling Up*.

13. Vance, *Elon Musk*.

14. Collins and Hansen, *Great by Choice*.

15. Turner, interview.

16. http://www.doseofleadership.com/20-inspirational-theodore-roosevelt-quotes/; http://www.theodorerooseveltcenter.org/Learn-About-TR/TR-Quotes?page=3.

17. Ragovin, interview.

18. Joseph Bellezzo, in-person interview with Ryan Berman, May 25, 2016.

CHAPTER 7: IDENTIFY FEARS

1. Reed Timmer, phone interview with Ryan Berman, July 7, 2016.

2. Brian Krans, *A Constant Suicide* (Davenport, IA: Rock Town Press, 2007).

3. David and Congleton, "Emotional Agility."

4. Loretta Hidalgo, in-person interview with Ryan Berman, February 26, 2016.

5. Jonathan Salem Baskin, "The Internet Didn't Kill Blockbuster, The Company Did It to Itself," *Forbes*, November 8, 2013, https://www.forbes.com/sites/jonathansalembaskin/2013/11/08/the-internet-didnt-kill-blockbuster-the-company-did-it-to-itself/#592c791b6488.

6. Geoffrey Precourt, "Turner Finding: Netflix #1 US TV network," WARC, February 2016, https://www.warc.com/Content/8df95baf-536e-40b2-b6fd-e3735c9bcb04.

7. Gerstner, *Who Says Elephants Can't Dance*.

8. Neil Blumenthal and David Gilboa, Warby Parker cofounders, Summit at Sea presentation, November 2015.

9. Mildenhall, "Fearless Marketing Drives AirBnB."

10. Grant, *Originals*.

11. Jack Williams, in-person interview with Ryan Berman, December 19, 2016.

12. Statista, "Revenue of Royal Caribbean from 1988 to 2017 (in billions U.S. dollars)," https://www.statista.com/statistics/224273/royal-caribbean-cruises-revenue/; "The World's Largest Public Companies," *Forbes*, June 2018, https://www.forbes.com/companies/royal-caribbean-cruises/.

13. Nicole Laporte, "HBO to Netflix: Bring It On," *Fast Company*, April 7, 2015, https://www.fastcompany.com/3044284/bring-it-on.

14. Robert J. Dolan, *The Black & Decker Corporation (A): Power Tools Division*, Harvard Business School Case 595-057, March 1995 (Revised March 2001).

15. John W. Gardner, *Self-Renewal: The Individual and the Innovative Society* (New York: W.W. Norton & Company Inc., 1981).

16. Assaraf, interview.

17. Cox-Martin, interview.

18. Jones, interview.

CHAPTER 8: COMMIT TO A PURPOSE

1. Vance, *Elon Musk*.

2. Vance, *Elon Musk*.

3. Michael Coren, "Facebook's Global Expansion No Longer Has Its Mission Statement Standing in the Way," Quartz, June 22, 2017, https://qz.com/1012461/facebook-changes-its-mission-statement-from-ing-its-mission-statement-from-sharing-making-the-world-more-open-and-connected-to-build-community-and-bring-the-world-closer-together/.

4. Jeremy Cowart, "Purpose Hotel: Change the World in Your Sleep," Kickstarter, October 2016, https://www.kickstarter.com/projects/thepurposehotel/ purpose-hotel-change-the-world-in-your-sleep.

5. Hiroko Tabuchi, "How CVS Quit Smoking and Grew Into a Health Care Giant," *The New York Times*, July 11, 2015, https://www.nytimes.com/2015/07/12/business/how-cvs-quit-smoking-and-grew-into-a-health-care-giant.html.

6. Simon Sinek, *Start With Why: How Great Leaders Inspire Everyone to Take Action* (New York: Penguin, 2009).

7. Nathan Smith, email interview with Ryan Berman, March 2016.

8. "How Persil Freed the Kids," WARC, May 4, 2016, https://www.warc.com/ newsandopinion/news/how_persil_freed_the_kids/36683.

9. Gilbert, interview.

10. "Why B Corps Matter," B Corps, http://www.bcorporation.net/what-are-b-corps/ why-b-corps-matter.

11. Gilbert, interview.

12. Ryan, interview.

13. Ryan, interview.

14. Kantar Millward Brown, "Brand Stability: 10 Year Trends," 2015, http://www. millwardbrown.com/brandz/top-global-brands/2015/10-year-results/10-year-trends

15. Jim Stengel, *Grow* (New York: Random House, 2011).

16. Kantar Millward Brown, "Brand Stability: 10 Year Trends," 2015.

CHAPTER 9: EXECUTE YOUR ACTION

1. Leon C. Megginson (paraphrasing Charles Darwin), "Key to Competition Is Management," *Petroleum Management*, Volume 36, Number 1, 1964, https:// quoteinvestigator.com/2014/05/04/adapt/.

2. Williams, interview.

3. Spero, interview.

4. "Gartner Reveals Top Predictions for IT Organizations and Users in 2017 and Beyond," October 2016, https://www.gartner.com/newsroom/id/3482117.

5. John Paul Titlow, "How Fender Is Reinventing Online Guitar Lessons for the Age of Distraction," *Fast Company*, July 6, 2017, https://www.fastcompany.com/40437554/ fender-reinvents-online-guitar-lessons-for-the-digitally-distracted.

6. "Global Advertising Consumers Trust Real Friends & Virtual Strangers the Most," Nielsen, July 7, 2009, http://www.nielsen.com/us/en/insights/news/2009/global-advertising-consumers-trust-real-friends-and-virtual-strangers-the-most.html.

7. Bruce Glassman, "Destination 2017: San Diego," Worth.com, http://www.worth.com/ destinations-2017-san-diego/.

8. Koch, interview.

9. Godin, *All Marketers Tell Stories.*

10. Salesforce Canada, "The Psychology of Sales Marketing and the Human Kind," Salesforce, May 1, 2015, https://www.salesforce.com/ca/blog/2015/04/psychology-of-sales.html.

11. Christopher Donnelly and Renato Scaff, "Who Are the Millennial Shoppers? And What Do They Really Want?" Accenture Outlook, https://www.accenture.com/us-en/insight-outlook-who-are-millennial-shoppers-what-do-they-really-want-retail.

12. Jay Baer, email interview with Ryan Berman, October 2017.

13. Eddie Tomalin, "80% of Millennials Will Watch a TV Show After Watching a Promo Shared with Them Online," *Unruly,* April 29, 2015, https://unruly.co/news/article/2015/04/29/80-of-millennials-will-watch-a-tv-show-after-watching-a-promo-shared-with-them-online/.

14. Jonah Berger, *Contagious: Why Things Catch On* (New York: Simon & Shuster, 2013).

15. Williams, interview.

16. Williams, interview.

CONCLUSION: YOUR ULTIMATE RETURN ON COURAGE

1. Steve Wilhite, interview with Ryan Berman, August 23, 2016.

2. https://www.linkedin.com/in/steven-wilhite-50114a40/

3. Wilhite, interview.

EPILOGUE

1. Deniz Yalim, "Letting Go Quotes: Moving On and Be Grateful Right Now," BayArt, February 5, 2017, https://bayart.org/letting-go-quotes-moving-on-and-be-grateful-right-now/.

GLOSSARY OF TERMS

BELIEVERSHIP: The core leadership team whose sole goal is to make Believers in all directions; make Believers out of your board, employees, and customers.

BUSINESS APOCALYPSE: Current landscape of companies dealing with external and internal factors inhibiting them from successfully transforming forward.

CALL FOR ACTION: A critical component one needs to bake inside a successful purpose. A call for action, not simply a call to action, gives your staff a meaningful reason to stick around to make good on the mission. It ignites and unites external Believers around your higher purpose.

CHEERLEADERSHIP: Within an organization, ineffective leaders often become cheerleaders, which creates Fake Believers versus true Believers.

CHIEF BELIEF OFFICER: The company's living, breathing raisons d'être. These culture-setters are the face of the company and a reason others buy in and believe.

CHIEF MEANINGFUL OFFICER: The ultimate goal of this role (usually a company's chief marketing officer) is to create meaningful products, services, and messages for their customers.

COURAGE BRAND: A brand that willingly addresses its business fears by gathering enough knowledge, building faith, and taking swift action.

COURAGE CREDO: Your 30,000-foot courage manifesto.

COVER AND MOVE: "Cover" your current business model while you work to "move" toward your next revenue stream or innovation, all under your existing purpose.

DO LEADERSHIP: Sibling of thought leadership. The precise execution of ideas.

EXPERIMENTAL TASK FORCE (ETF): Where most of your company remains ground soldiers, this mission-focused internal "special forces" squad gets the time, space, and budget to tackle possible future problems. It is empowered to unearth industry blind spots or recommend new innovative revenue-generating opportunities before your competitors do.

FAKE BELIEVERS: Nonbelievers in your organization who may become toxic employees. You need to convert them to Believers or move on from them.

INDUSTRY BLIND SPOT: Undeclared and unforeseen companies that are not yet on your radar. They have the potential to be the industry fear of tomorrow for an entire category.

NARROWCASTING: Narrowly casting your point of view to those aligned promoters who, in turn, will take your message and become walking vessels called upon to broadcast your gospel to the masses.

NOISE PER MINUTE: The amount of content per minute currently permeating consumers.

P.R.I.C.E.: A five-step process you can follow to shape your company's Central Courage System. The acronym stands for *Prioritize through Values, Rally Believers, Identify Fears, Commit to a Purpose,* and *Execute Your Action.*

PURPOSE ELASTICITY: A purpose that can stretch to cover new revenue streams you put into the market that keep the company relevantly evolving.

"RALLY CRY IN YOUR WHY" PURPOSE: This "higher-calling" purpose unites and ignites your internal Believers and motivates internal staff as much as external prospects. Ultimately, it gives your employees a reason to stick around.

RETURN ON COURAGE: The return a business, being, or brand gets from tapping into and activating their courage. Look to maximize your return on investment with a Return on Courage.

INDEX

A

Accenture, 28

action, taking, 61–65

ad blockers, 24

addressing fears, 131–34

Advanstar, 176–77

advertising

    overview, 23–25, 170–72

    passion in, 178–79

    point of view in, 173–76

    precision in, 176–78

    promoters, role of, 179–83

advocacy, 171, 174, 198–99

Airbnb, 136

alignment of message, 119–20

Alp, Nicholas, 30

amazing content, creating, 172

Amazon, 144, 153, 168–69

Apple, 193–94

Army values, 90–91

aspirational content, creating, 172

Assaraf, John, 82, 142–43

authentic content, creating, 171–72

Avery, Jill, 40, 57–58

awareness of values and purpose, 197–98

B

Babin, Leif, 58, 111

Baer, Jay, 180

Baskin, Jonathan Salem, 134

believers

    Believership, 112–15, 168, 189–90

    Chief Belief Officers, 115–16

    conviction in, 198

    fake, 123–24, 194

    making, 116–22

    rallying believers worksheet, 123–24

Believership, 112–15, 168, 189–90

Bellezzo, Joe, 122

Berger, Jonah, 180

Berman, Ryan, 201

Bezos, Jeff, 98

B Lab, 156–58

Black & Decker, 140–42

Blanchard, Ken, 112

Blockbuster, 134

blocking ads, 24

Blumenthal, Neil, 135

Boss, Jeff, 47, 49, 71, 78

Boston Consulting Group, 20

brain, emotional, 30–31

brand loyalty, 25

Brandon, Dave, 11

Branson, Richard, 54

Brown, Brené, 39, 51

Buddy Media, 72, 121

business apocalypse

    death of companies, 20–30

    failure to evolve, 32–33

    fear of change, 30–32

    four truths of, 19–20

    overview, 17–19

    rate of change, 33–36

business culture, 25–26, 74

C

cancer, courage in face of, 18–19

Cardone, Grant, 6, 52–53

Category One brands, 166–67

cautionary descenders, 202

Cecchetto, Carlo, 79

Central Courage System, 85–88,
    189–91

central nervous system, 81–83, 143

Chambers, John, 23

change

    external factors, 23–25

    fear of, 30–32

    internal factors, 25–30

    rate of, 33–36

    responding to, 199

    staying relevant, 32–33

Chapin-Bayley, Patricia, 79–80

cheerleadership, 112

Chief Belief Officer, 115–16

Chief Meaningful Officer, 196

clarity of message, 119–20

clarity of values, 197–98

Collins, Jim, 22–23, 85–86, 120

committing to purpose

    being different, 160

    emotional purposes, 158–60

    overview, 151–54, 161–62, 209

    purposefulness, importance of,
        155–58

    truthfulness, importance of,
        154–55

    worksheet, 163–64

communication, in internal change
    strategy, 27

compassionate courage, 39

competition, 23–25

confidence, 200

Congleton, Christina, 92, 131

consumer, role of, 23–25

contacts in social media, 181

content marketing

    overview, 169–72

    passion in, 178–79

    point of view in, 173–76

    precision in, 176–78

promoters, role of, 179–83

conviction, 198

Cook, Tim, 93

core values

assessment of, 211–13

awareness of, 197–98

knowing, 91–94

living, 99–104

overview, 89–91

prioritizing, 94–99

prioritizing through values worksheet, 107–10

Values Arrow, 104–5

corporate culture, 25–26, 74

courage

compassionate, 39

effect on others, 200

employer, 39–40

encouraged, 39

extreme, 38–39

faith, basing on, 57–61

knowledge, basing on, 53–57

redefining, 51–53

taking action, 61–65

"Courage as a Skill" (Reardon), 45

Courage Brands

defined, 64–65

description of, 189–91, 196–97

traits of, 205–6

transformation into, 85–86

courage myths

impulsivity, 44–46

innateness, 46–48

others have courage, 38–40

overview, 37–38

recklessness, 40–42

risky solo journeys, 42–44

unrelated to daily life, 48–49

Courageous, 158

cover and move principle, 168–69

Cowart, Jeremy, 152

Cox-Martin, Emily, 81–82, 143

Crayola, 153

CVS Pharmacy, 152

D

daily life, courage in, 48–49

Dali, Salvador, 36

data, value of, 55–57

David, Susan, 92, 131

deadlines, 34

death of companies

external factors, 23–25

general discussion, 20–23

internal factors, 25–30

delegating tasks, 118–19

Deloitte 2018 Millennial Survey, 35

DeWalt, 141–42

differential purpose, 160

Dollar Shave Club, 115

Domino's, 10–13

Dove, 153

Doyle, J. Patrick, 11–12

Dubin, Michael, 115

E

Eddie Bauer, 73–74

Elon Musk: Tesla, SpaceX, and the Quest for a Fantastic Future (Vance), 77, 151–52

"Emotional Agility" (David and Congleton), 92

emotional brain, 30–31

emotional purpose, 158–60

emotions, buying decisions based on, 178

employees

    believers, creating, 116–22

    fake believers, 123–24

    internal change, factors affecting, 25–30

    talent, recruiting, 69–70

    team, building, 70–75

    training for courage, 78–83

    trusting and empowerment of, 34–35

    turnover time, 35–36

employer courage, 39–40

empowerment, 34–35

encouraged courage, 39

enemy, knowing, 157

Enge, Brian, 28–29

entrepreneurship, decline in, 22

ETF (experimental task force), 143–44, 167–68, 169, 190

Everlane, 98

evolving to stay relevant, 32–33

Ewing Marion Kauffman Foundation, 22

executing action. *See also* marketing

    cover and move principle, 168–69

    new offerings, 166–68

    overview, 165–66, 210

    worksheet, 185–88

experience, knowledge from, 54–57

experimental task force (ETF), 143–44, 167–68, 169, 190

experiments, knowledge from, 54

expertise, role in decision making, 45

external hiring, 35

extreme courage, 38–39

Extreme Ownership: How Navy SEALs Lead and Win (Willink and Babin), 58

F

Facebook, 152

failure, fear of, 142

Fain, Richard, 137

faith, basing decisions on, 57–61

fake believers, 123–24, 194

fears

    addressing, 131–34

    of change, 30–32

    experimental task force, combating with, 143–44

    identifying fear worksheet, 147–49

    industry, 134–37

    overview, 129–31

perception, 140–42

personal, 142–43

product, 137–39

service, 139–40

Feld, Kenneth, 133

Fender, 63–64, 114, 169

Fishtank, 6

Fortune 500 companies, 19

Fraggle Rock (TV show), 176

Fraser, Drew, 115

Frazier, Kenneth, 136

G

Gardner, John W., 142

Gates, Bill, 69

Gerstner, Lou, 26, 76, 135

Gilbert, Jay Coen, 30, 48, 72, 155–57

Gilboa, David, 135

Gladwell, Malcolm, 45

Godin, Seth, 85, 175

Google, 29, 55, 118, 167–68

Gracias, Antonio, 77

Grant, Adam, 43, 136

Great by Choice (Collins), 22–23

Guillies, Wendy, 22

H

Harnish, Verne, 80, 118–19

Harrah's Resort Southern California, 98–99

Harris, Jared, 28

HBO, 139–40

Herbert, Coleman, 39

Hidalgo, Loretta, 132–33

hiring talented employees, 69–70

Hsieh, Tony, 28

I

i.d.e.a., 6, 98, 176–77

identifying fears

addressing fears, 131–34

experimental task force, combating fears with, 143–44

industry fears, 134–37

overview, 129–31, 209

perception fears, 140–42

personal fears, 142–43

product fears, 137–39

service fears, 139–40

worksheet, 147–49

impulsivity, 44–46

industry blind spots, 135–36, 169

industry fears, 134–37

innateness of courage, 46–48

innovation, attitudes towards, 28

instinct, acting on, 45–46, 79

internal change, 25–30

irresponsibility, 157

J

JetBlue, 100–103

Jobs, Steve, 69, 115

Jones, Evan, 63–64, 114, 143

journey of courage, 42–44

K

Kantar Millward Brown, 160

Kiely, Katz, 117

Kline, Greg, 56

Knight, Bobby, 81

knowing values, 91–94

knowledge, basing courage on, 41, 53–57

Koch, Greg, 76, 173–75

Krans, Brian, 130

L

Lao-tzu, 202

LDRSHIP, 90–91

leadership, 112–15

learning courage, 46–47

legacy brands, 14, 20–22

Lencioni, Patrick, 114

LinkedIn, 170

Littrell, Erin, 55

living values, 99–104

Lowry, Adam, 114–15, 158–59

M

Marcario, Rose, 156

Marino, JT, 113

marketing

overview, 169–72

passion in, 178–79

point of view in, 173–76

precision in, 176–78

promoters, role of, 179–83

Martin, Roger, 31–33, 56

McCord, Patty, 69

McKee, Steve, 22

Messner Vetere Berger McNamee Schmetterer, 4–6

Method, 114–15, 158–60

micromanaging, 34–35

Mildenhall, Jonathan, 36

Millennials, 117, 180, 198

Musk, Elon, 70, 77, 119, 122, 151–52

N

narrowcasting, 181–83, 206

Netflix, 134

New Oxford American Dictionary, 37

new products and services, creating, 166–68

Nhat Hanh, Thich, 71

O

Outliers: The Story of Success (Gladwell), 45

P

Page, Larry, 70

parasympathetic nervous system, 81–82

Park, Daehee, 58–59, 96, 113, 115

passion, 178–79

Patagonia, 156

Pearson, Mike, 54–55, 70

perception fears, 10, 11, 140–42

Persil, 154–55

personal fears, 142–43

personal responsibility, 28–29

personal risk, 27

persuasive messages, 170–72

Pilant, Darrell, 98–99

Plepler, Richard, 140

point of view, 173–76

Positioning: The Battle for Your Mind (Ries and Trout), 58

positive attitude, importance of, 76–77

positive reinforcement, 121

practicing courage, 46–47, 78–83

precision of execution, 176–78

P.R.I.C.E. process, 87, 207–10. *See also specific steps*

pride, change complicated by, 29–30

principles of courage
    overview, 67–69
    talent, 69–70
    team, 70–75
    tenacity, 75–78
    training, 78–83

prioritizing through values
    knowing values, 91–94
    living values, 99–104
    overview, 89–91, 208
    prioritizing values, 94–99
    Values Arrow, 104–5
    worksheet, 107–10

product fears, 10–11, 137–39

products. *See also* marketing
    cover and move principle, 168–69
    creating new, 166–68

promoters, role of, 179–83

Purcell, Thomas, 18–19, 86

purpose
    awareness of, 197–98
    being different, 160
    committing to, 161–62
    committing to purpose worksheet, 163–64
    emotional, 158–59
    overview, 151–54
    purposefulness, importance of, 155–58
    truthfulness, importance of, 154–55

purpose elasticity, 161, 209

purposefulness, importance of, 155–58

Purpose Hotel, 152

Q

Qualcomm, 31–33

R

Ragovin, Jeff, 72, 117, 121

Raine, Burke, 62–63

"rally cry in your why" purpose, 153–54, 158, 205

rallying believers
    Believership, 112–15
    Chief Belief Officers, 115–16
    creating believers, 116–22
    fake believers, 123–24
    overview, 111–12, 208
    worksheet, 125–28

Reardon, Kathleen, 45, 47

recklessness, 40–42

recruiting talent, 69–70

relationships, cultivating, 120–21

repetition, making believers through, 119–20

reputation, 57

resilience, 75–76, 77–78

respecting teams, 118–19

retail, death of companies in, 20–22

return on courage, 197–200

return on investment (ROI), maximizing, 13–14, 197–200

Ries, Al, 58

Ringling Bros., 133

Rising Strong (Brown), 51

risk

    courage, balancing with, 14–15

    courage myths, 42–44

    personal, 27

Robin Hood Brands, 28

Rodriguez, Manny, 27

ROI (return on investment), maximizing, 13–14, 197–200

Roosevelt, Teddy, 62, 121

Roth, Rich, 5

Royal Caribbean Cruises, 137–39, 166–67

Rubino, Mike, 49

Russell Reynolds Associates, 35

Ryan, Eric, 114–15, 158–60

S

Sandberg, Sheryl, 75

Sandoval, Claudia, 58–61

Scaling Up (Harnish), 80, 118–19

Scholes, Myron, 14–15

Schopenhauer, Arthur, 58

seeing is believing, 121–22

sense of urgency, 62–63, 205

service fears, 139–40

services, creating new, 166–68. *See also* marketing

Silvestri, Phil, 5

Sinek, Simon, 153

Slater, Steven, 100–103

Smith, Nathan, 153

social media

    content marketing, 170–72

    feedback on, 63

    promoters, 179–83

Southwest, 170

speed, importance of, 62–63

Spero, Jason, 29, 57, 99–100, 167–68

start-ups, 25

Stengel 50, 161

Stengel, Jim, 161

Stone Brewing, 173–75

storm chasing, 129–30

stress inoculation, 47

Subway, 5

support system, 43–44

suppressing fears, 131–34

sympathetic nervous system, 81–82, 143

T

talent, recruiting, 69–70

teaching courage, 46–48

teams

Believership, 112–15

building, 70–75

creating believers, 116–22

experimental task force, 143–44,
167–68, 169, 190

support from, 43–44

10,000-hour rule, 45

tenacity, 75–78

Thiel, Peter, 119

Timmer, Reed, 129–30

training for courage, 46–47, 78–83

Treasurer, Bill, 46

TripAdvisor, 42

Trout, Jack, 58

Truman, Harry, 72

trust

importance of, 114

in internal change strategy, 27

lack of, effect on turnaround
time, 34–35

truthful purpose, 154–55

Tuft & Needle, 58–59, 96, 113

turnaround time, 34–35

Turner, Andrew, 41, 120

turnover time, 34, 35–36

V

values

assessment of, 211–13

knowing, 91–94

living, 99–104

overview, 89–91

prioritizing, 94–99

prioritizing through values worksheet, 107–10

Values Arrow, 104–5, 153

Vance, Ashlee, 77, 151–52

W

Wallach, Russell, 74–75

Walshe, Peter, 161

Weiner, Russell, 10–13, 40

Who Says Elephants Can't Dance?
(Gerstner), 26

why statement, 153

Wilhite, Steve, 193–96

Williams, Jack, 137–39, 166–67

Williams, Tyler, 98, 182

willing ascenders, 201–2

Willink, Jocko, 58, 111

Wilson, E. O., 55–56

word of mouth, 180

worksheets

committing to purpose, 163–64

executing action, 185–88

identifying fears, 147–49

prioritizing through values,
107–10

rallying believers, 125–28

Z

Zappos, 98, 153, 182

zombie apocalypse, 32–33

ABOUT THE AUTHOR

RYAN BERMAN IS the founder of Courageous, a creative consultancy that develops Courage Brands™ and trains organizations through Courage Bootcamp. Working with brands like Caesars Entertainment, Major League Baseball, PUMA, Subway, U.S. Ski & Snowboard Association, and UNICEF, Berman developed the concept that courage can give any brand a competitive advantage.

In addition to Courage Bootcamp, Berman founded Sock Problems, a charitable sock company that supports causes around the world by "socking" problems and spreading awareness. Previously, he was the cofounder of i.d.e.a., an integrated marketing agency based in San Diego.

Berman has been featured in Entrepreneur.com, Inc.com, *Ad Age, PRWeek,* and podcasts like Creative Mornings and Hustle & Deal Flow. He was named one of San Diego's "Top 40 under 40" by *SD Metro* and is a recognized business and leadership speaker.

Berman is an avid soccer player and lives in San Diego with his wife and two kids. You can catch up with him on Twitter @RyanBerman or on LinkedIn @CourageousBrands.